BOM BOMBSHELL

When the world

you created goes
NUCLEAR

Kate Foxton

Copyright © 2018 Kate Foxton

All rights reserved.

This book came about because of an amazing Roar of Unicorns.

You wonderful bunch of women made the very darkest moments of my journey so much brighter. I could not have got through these last months without your amazing and unwavering support, encouragement and wise advice. Lord, did I need advice.

Your humour made my many visits to the last cubicle in the Ladies Toilet at work much shorter and less snotty. I am forever a fan of Facebook Messenger, and Wi-Fi in toilets. Every single one of you is in my heart forever. Thank you.

In addition, my unwavering love and gratitude go to these Unicorns:

Vicky, for coming up with the title of the blog, as well as many others that were unprintable. You also spawned ODFOP. In short you are a creative genius and I am lucky you aren't asking for royalties.

Sophie for making me believe I may actually be ok at writing, and for nagging me about hashtags, even when you're on holiday.

Chantelle for organising me, focussing me, and making me take out the cartoons that would have otherwise got me sued.

My fabulous **sister Fo**, for her unending cheerleading, encouragement and love, even when my life has been a picnic compared to hers. And also for being the brains **and** the brawn of our business raw2ROAR. Without you Fo, it would still be just a nice idea.

CONTENTS

I. THE NUCLEAR OPTION
II. THE POST-APOCALYPTIC WEEK
III. HOAM WRECKER AND A ROAR OF UNICORNS
IV. A POTTED HISTORY OF MY LIFE PRE-ODFOP
V. ODFOP BECOMES LODGER ODFOP
VI. THE THUNDERSTORM OF FATE
VII. THE JOEY TEXT
VIII. I HAVE FOUND MY ROAR
IX. POTTED ODFOP
X. PLANNING THE WEDDING... THEN NOT
XI. THE WEDDING WAS ON... THEN OFF... THEN ON
XII. MY TERRORISING "KINDNESS"
XIII. ODFOP – GRAND MASTER OF CUNNING
XIV. ODFOP AND OTHER ANIMALS PART 1
XV. ODFOP AND OTHER ANIMALS PART 2
XVI. SHOPPING SANS ODFOP
XVII. HOLIDAYS PAST - ICELAND
XVIII. NEW YEAR – NEW ME
XIX. IT HAS BEGUN
XX. THE "C" WORD
XXI. THIS OLD HOUSE
XXII. ODFOP HAS A GIRLFRIEND
XXIII. ODFOP – GASLIGHTER EXTRAORDINAIRE
XXIV. ODFOP THE CULT LEADER

Introduction

Hi there. I'm Kate. I'm the wrong side of 50, I have a BMI of 42 and as I take it now, a resting pulse of 118. I am terrified and (I am pretty sure) heartbroken.

Adrenalin junkies, WTF? This is hideous, why would you get like this by *choice*?

My relationship, which has lasted a third of my entire life, has broken down and I am being forced to start again. Alone.

.......ish.

It's just me, and my 14 or so furred and feathered dependants.

I feel simultaneously like I am being pushed over a precipice where I can't see the bottom and chained at the bottom of a black pit with only a pinprick of light far up above.

I know, right?

My brain and body are metaphorically clinging to the floor, eyes tightly shut waiting for this dreadful paralysing **terror** to pass. Like me at 14, first experience with alcohol, drunk on a cocktail of Cinzano Bianco, crème de menthe, Advocaat and cherry brandy – (we called it a Pan-Galactic

Gargleblaster – like from Hitchhikers Guide to the Galaxy)

Exactly like that.

Except without the vomiting through my nose and my parents not letting me out for 3 months.

The idea of this blog came from my husband, actually (hereafter known as ODFOP – to be further explained).

A few days after I noticed ODFOP "working" all night on his laptop (he has a very undemanding job) I accidentally slipped while holding his iPad and it happened to open his emails. While putting it back on the bedside cabinet, I noticed his emails were in folder called MWD. I opened an email in that file and clicked on a link that said "Taniapuss" had a response for him.

I knew he dealt with people all over the world with his job. Maybe some unfortunate professional had been named Taniapuss by innocent parents who just like the sound of the name, or it meant *Goddess of Beauty* in Sanskrit?

I discovered that Taniapuss did not want to buy his company's software, but that she was responding to a message from him where he had disclosed the most intimate and personal details and criticisms he had of me.

All to a 28-year-old blonde woman called Taniapuss (apparently) whose profile picture was her vulva.

He had joined a sex website called Marriedwomen.co.uk. and had been messaging maybe a dozen different women. It seemed to be doing him the *world* of good to offload his deepest and most private thoughts, whilst simultaneously and *very* enthusiastically informing the young lady of what he would like to do to her profile picture *in person,* as it were.

As it seemed to be so unbelievably cathartic and stimulating for him to talk intimately to strangers, I have decided to do the same.

My aim in this blog is to be absolutely down-to-the-bone honest, and hopefully entertaining, but mostly it's to help me find the courage to start again on my own.

If someone else is watching (you, my one lovely reader) then I shall be spurred on to make those leaps of faith, to feel that fear but do it anyway, and to lose the weight so I can see my toes again.

Be assured (or disappointed) there will be no photos of Labia Majora or Minora in this blog....

I. THE NUCLEAR OPTION

There I was, reading my husband's emails. Something I never thought I would *ever* do. It felt deceitful, voyeuristic and forbidden - and I felt hideously guilty.

There is something you should know about me. I am an open book.

An open book with short easy to read words, printed in large type that gives the plot away on the first page.

I would *love* to be mysterious and secretive. I'd even be delighted to be a little reticent or reserved. I just do not possess the skillset.

I'm pretty sure anyone within 50 feet of me knows what I am thinking, as I am either saying it out loud or my face portrays it quite clearly.

ODFOP has all my passwords, PIN's, everything - I never cared about being open - with him I *wanted* to be **even more** open, because I wanted *him* to open-up - to me.

He has the reticent skillset, in spades.

I digress. I was desperate to read everything, while simultaneously wanting to run away and scrub my brain clean.

He was dissatisfied with practically every aspect of my being. I had never seen him be so open and expressive, ever. He was telling this complete stranger how I'd let myself go, our sex life was boring because I was self-conscious, and that we had nothing to talk about anymore.

I learned so much more about what he was really feeling about me in those few messages, than he had ever expressed to me in the seventeen years we had been together. I had opened Pandora's box. I had always wanted to know what he was thinking. Lucky, lucky me.

I was struck by the intense burning heat of my cheeks and the speed at which this screaming, swirling, aching, void was growing inside, filling every fat, ugly millimetre of me.

He wrote about how beautiful she was. How beautiful her labia were to him. He wrote explicit details of what he wanted to do to them. As hot stinging tears formed, my eyes changed focus and I saw my reflection in his iPad. My double chin, my down turned mouth, my permanent frown line. No makeup, hair frizzy and not done.

No wonder he hated me. I was disgusting. I had driven him to this.

Shaking, I put his iPad down and went and stood in the kitchen. I just stood there, rooted to the spot, unable to move. My mind too overwhelmed to think.

After I don't know how long of staring at nothing at all, adrenalin and shock subsided, and I gained some sense. I grabbed my iPad and typed in www.marriedwomen.co.uk.

Holy crap! Who knew these websites existed?! Ok, fair enough, apparently a LOT of people do.

It was like a freak show. Pictures and messages flashing on the screen in bright colours. It enthusiastically promised plentiful meetings with "like-minded people" looking for no strings attached sex. It flashed up excitedly

"FREE TO JOIN!!"

"don't join until you're ready for sex with attractive strangers!" and

"you could be contacted for sex within **minutes** of joining!"

Photos of very normal looking people in not very attractive amateur poses mingled with HUGE erect penises, grotesquely over enlarged boobs, and much older women in really heavy makeup, leering at the camera with saggy *everything* confidently displayed.

Photos of vulvas and penises were flashing up saying "I'm local and I'm ready to receive you NOW!"

Mesmerised, I clicked on the joining page and filled it out with some appropriately fake details and pressed Enter.

The next page said that while it was indeed free to join - it was £2 to read, and £2 to send a message to a "like minded, ready-for-kinky-unattached-sex-with-you-right-now-person".

He was spending *money* on this?

I looked on some of the profiles. I was shocked at how these "young women" - all in their 20's, all in low paying but very proper jobs (think teaching assistant, care worker, nursery school helper, shop assistant) all lovely (those that had photos of their face instead of their reproductive organs) would or could:

a) ever need to be on such a website to get male attention; and

b) afford £2 to send and receive a message?

I went back to reading ODFOP's messages.

They were very detailed and explicit, very complimentary of these young women and he was openly grateful they were interested in him. I skipped through the detailed fantasy paragraphs - I wanted to see what he honestly thought about me, no matter how bad.

He had a **lot** to say. So very private and intimate things. The cold and detached way he described me

11

and our failed marriage, repeatedly took my breath away.

The emotions that were swirling round me were fighting, all of them aiming for pole position. Jealousy, guilt, disgust, grief, self-pity, with extra lashings of self-loathing. Each surfacing for a moment before being pushed out and replaced by another.

I also couldn't shake the uncomfortable feeling that it was just all a bit, well - *seedy*.

He had posted normal photos of himself, and one was a picture of us and I was just cropped out. Of course, he wouldn't have a photo of both of us on this kind of website, but it stung that it was a happy photo of us together which I had loved.

He looked over 50, a bit portly - like an average middle-aged man. Not tall, not muscly, but bespectacled, bearded with receding greying hair and a round face. Objectively, he wasn't someone you think "ooh, handsome". Not unless you were married to him.

I imagined his face being flashed up on the News, he'd been caught for exposing himself to young women in a park - and he looked like a creepy, dirty old man. Same photo that I had loved up until now - but now he looked deeply disturbed and dangerous. I was horrified. How could he think it was ok to talk to people like that - young girls that he didn't know? Like using a prostitute - these women are vulnerable and need safety, not some selfish wanker taking advantage of that vulnerability for their own selfish one-sided pleasure.

And then it got worse...

He also had posted a picture of his erect penis.... My stomach flipped, and stampeding elephants swept through me again.

I could see our bedroom furniture in the photo! How could he?? It was abusive and predatory. Oh my God. My husband was a predator.

Part of me also thought "You fucking idiot. A cock shot on the internet and you've put your real name, your work email address, **and** photos of your face?"

I continued to read the messages from these young women. There was no mistaking that they, i.e."Iluvurcock_123", "cumonmeplz", "Taniapuss" (aka The Vulva) were very politely welcoming my husband's attention.

Yes, they preferred older men. Yes, they thought he was handsome, and yes, they were on the website because they too didn't want the hassle of a relationship - they just wanted no strings attached sex. They generally, quite coquettishly, approved of his explicit fantasies with him.

"Coquettish" is not an expected word to think when reading something by a person whose profile says they like dogging, anal fisting and water sports - but they were exceptionally well typed and polite. You also don't expect someone who calls themselves cumonmeplz to know the difference between "your" and "you're", and when to use a semi-colon.

The response from The Vulva replying to ODFOP's message (which was both a therapy session and a full and graphic fantasy) was "well, that was a lovely message to read on my lunch hour – please tell me a little more".

After about 30 minutes of flicking through his messages, I had emotionally shut down.

My brain acted like a bouncer at a nightclub "Nope, we're too full. I'll let Hot Swirling Pain and Stinging Tears in because they're regulars who quietly get drunk in the corner, but the rest of you loud screaming thoughts look like trouble so you're not coming in".

As the day progressed, the numbness began to wear off. The screaming, aching hot swirl of emptiness gathered strength like a tornado - sending me searing hot flashes of lightning to remind me that my carefully curated world was now a bombsite. Hot tears formed and poured freely off my chin and onto the floor.

Randomly, a thought flashed through my mind – good friends were coming for dinner the following night.

Oh shit.

It was supposed to be a fun filled evening with wine and conversation flowing easily.

A massive wave of nausea washed over me. Tears and Swirling Emptiness had clearly booked themselves in for at least the weekend - there was no way on earth I could be Bright and Breezy by tomorrow night.

I had to talk to her – this wasn't something that could be explained away in a casual text. The dinner had been planned for a long time and we'd all been looking forward to it.

I shakily sent a text asking for her to call me when she was free – she texted back to say she'd call in 10 minutes. I had 10 minutes to think about what I was going to say. WTF was I going to say?? I couldn't chirpily say "hey there, sorry for the late notice, so you mind if we rearrange dinner plans? No, nothing serious, just need to get this meltdown out of the way and potentially I may be burying my husband in the garden. I just won't have time to clean my nails and get the wine in. Yes, next Saturday should be fine."

I sat there staring blankly at the phone until it rang.

"hey lovey – everything alright?" were the words that undid me.

That familiar friendly voice, and suddenly I was now in the calm eye of the raging storm and she was there to pick me up with a cup of tea and a warm blanket. I started awkwardly but I blurted it all out – everything, sobbing and wailing as I spoke.

She was amazing. She listened without interruption to my blathering jumbled wails and simply said "well this just doesn't sound right".

Those six words stopped me in my tracks. Stopped the tears, stopped the aching void – gave me.... HOPE. Hope that I'd got it wrong, or it didn't exist, or that he *did* really love me - hope that it wasn't as bad as it felt it was.

All the signs that I had missed or ignored.

- The "innocent" jobs that paid very little.
- The preferring older men.
- The polite encouraging responses but never reciprocating or contributing to the fantasies.
- The £2 a message.
- ODFOP pleading to The Vulva to get a Hotmail account so they could continue their "discussions" off (premium rate) line. Her polite refusal, saying "she had credit to use up".

Of course! ODFOP was being scammed! How absolutely marvellous! Instantly I could see it as clear as day. The relief flooding through me was palpable.

They weren't real people!! Honestly, to anyone thinking with their brain and not their penis or broken heart, the signs were 10 feet tall, dressed in neon spandex and waving flags. And my gorgeous best friend had spotted it instantly. Thank God for her. My pain and tears had gone.

To be replaced apparently, by mild to middling hysteria.

Now my brain let everything flood in. I imagined two old men in a shed in Wales with two battered computers each. Bill turning to Bernard saying "Ay, Bern, this one wants to take me up the arse in Sainsbury's car park and then buy me a chicken burger" and Bernard saying "ooh, you lucky bugger, at least you get taken to dinner - the one I've got just wants to suck me toes through me fishnets and wear me shoes". They both look down at Bernard's size 12 battered old wellies, and chuckle.

This, I could handle.

But then, niggles started niggling. Uncomfortable thoughts came to my mind. Something wasn't right. I started to worry - about my poor husband.

What if he thinks he is going to meet The Vulva and he gets to the Travelodge to find a huge Russian man with a picture of his cock and he is blackmailed? Or beaten up? How much money had he already spent? From the number of messages, he had sent and received it must've already been £500. What if they say they need money and he sends it to them?

Suddenly, full and furious turmoil was back - this time it was fear for my poor, poor husband.

He was clearly trying to be validated by someone. He wanted to feel attractive and desirable, something I clearly hadn't done a good job on. He was lost, lonely and desperate and seeking approval from some wanker that was scamming him and probably laughing at ODFOP's therapeutic outpourings. Bastards. How could they be so cold towards my husband? Don't they know he finds it very hard to open up?? He has put himself out there as a genuine person looking for, well, my brain ignored what he was looking for and replaced it with "connection" – he was looking to connect with someone.

Oh my God what have I done to him? I thought I was doing him a favour, so he didn't have to look at my fat body - but he was craving attention. He never told me. Not once.

I had to protect him and tell him I can be everything he wants me to be. Now I know what he needs - I will be that for him and we can be happy again.

I needed to plan and do this right. Now, how could I alert ODFOP without having to confess that I'd read his emails?

My brain was aching. My head pounded, and my eyes were sore and swollen. I needed to resolve this, I couldn't let him carry on being so gullible. All I wanted to do was hug him tightly and sob how sorry I was.

He walked through the door and I was sitting in the dark – I hadn't even noticed. I made some dinner while my heart was pounding, and my stomach was in my ears – I still had no idea how to broach it all. It was so important, I couldn't risk messing this up. If I did it right, we would spend the rest of the evening cuddled up on the sofa and we will be in love again. Our friends could come around and it would be like it was many years ago. fun, love and laughter. Thank goodness.

We sat down on separate sofas and began to eat. My mouth took over while my brain was screaming "Noooo! Not yet! We don't know what to say yet!"

"can we talk for a few minutes?" My brain slapped its palm on its forehead "you idiot! Now what are you going to do?"

"if you want" he said while still watching the telly and eating.

I didn't know what to say next. Probably a full minute later he turned away from the television and looked at me for the first time since coming in.

It was not a look of love. It was a look of bored detachment. He put his plate down and picked his laptop up.

"I need to tell you something and I am not sure how to start. I have done something, and I think you will be angry with me, but I think I need to tell you anyway because I care about you"

"go on then" he said as he sat back and started his laptop up.

"I looked in your emails today" he froze for a nano-second and then carried on tapping his password in

"right?"

"I saw the emails from that website and the things that you were saying to them. I didn't look at them all, but I looked at some. I saw some of the things you said about me"

"right?"

"I am only telling you because I care about you. You are being scammed". I went on to explain all the 10 feet high signs that he was being scammed and he listened without saying a word – or looking at me. I told him how I was devastated that he disliked so much about me and he clearly didn't even like me let alone love me anymore.

His response was not what I hoped for.

He said he wasn't angry with me for reading his emails, he didn't mean for me to see what he had written about me, but he did mean it.

He meant it all.

He said he had been getting an inkling that all wasn't right with all these women, but he had not crystallised the evidence as quickly as I had, (I didn't mention that I hadn't either, and it was my clever best mate who had been the detective) and he could see that I was right. He said he had "probably made some poor choices in joining the website". It was like he was being told off at work for spending too much time playing solitaire.

Boom! A dirty bomb of words and tone that can't ever be unheard went off inside me and obliterated my world.

I was sitting there, silent, breathing and blinking - but in a gazillion screaming, terrified pieces.

He carried on logging in to his laptop and watching the television and didn't say another word to me that night.

He had pressed the button that said Nuclear Option and he didn't care.

II. The Post-Apocalyptic Week

I lay awake all that night thinking about everything and anything that wasn't what had just happened.

Of course, this whole situation hadn't appeared totally out of the blue. There had been many signs, possibly for years, that our relationship wasn't a very good match.

To help explain a little about how I got this far in my marriage/life without tackling any of these problems, let me introduce you one or two of a mini-me's that rule my life. think "Inside Out" by Pixar.

Lalala. Lalala wears rose tinted sunglasses, always has headphones round her neck, is incredibly good at all kinds of crafts and has a permanent coat-hanger-in-the-mouth kind of smile.

She's mostly in been in charge for the last 40 of my 50+ years. Life is lovely with Lalala. I am incredibly lucky, happy and safe with Lalala. Lalala can always see the positive in any situation or person, and I genuinely feel blessed that she is part of me.

Lalala also protects me from Upsetting Things.

Lalala is right there when The Upset first arrives in my head. Headphones on, lalalaing to the music, she will wrestle it into submission, drag it off to the Crafting Room and slam the door behind her with her foot.... The Upset will struggle and wriggle and try and be appropriately dealt with, but Lalala is good, and *very* experienced.

Sellotape is always already cut into neat pieces and sticking off the edge of the table. Bright wrapping paper, glue, glitter, pipe cleaners, empty loo rolls, plasticine, ribbon and tissue paper are all within easy reach. Her hands are a blur as she transforms the Upset into an unrecognisable masterpiece.

Think "masterpiece" as in the ones parents have to take home at the end of the nursery term.

Once she is satisfied that it's much prettier, unable to escape and no longer a threat, she'll stick it in a lead lined box, rivet it shut, slap a DO NOT OPEN sticker on it and throw it over a cliff.

The Craft Room is a mess and Lalala has a sweaty top lip and a slight twitch in one eye, but everything is fine. I've moved on and am slightly surprised to find I am thinking about kittens and knitting again, but I'm happy in a floaty and serene way.

ODFOP going Nuclear came under that category.

23

Thanks to Lalala, by the following morning I had practically forgotten about it.

I worked, tidied the house, made dinner and cheerily said "hi, how was your day?" when he came in that night.

It worked - for the first time in many months, we sat on the same sofa and chatted like a "normal couple".

He made some mildly amusing comments about someone on the television and I laughed my head off. I said, "ooh clever" and smiled at him when he got a question right on University Challenge.

Lalala was doing cartwheels down the corridor and sticking her photo in the "employee of the month" frame.

This carried on for most of the week. But, Thursday night was looming like a big loom. Thursday night had been in the diary for weeks and weeks and was drinks with some properly lovely girlfriends I used to work with.

There was one tiny HUGE problem.

One of them knew about me and ODFOP splitting up.

I had posted a "poor me" message on Facebook previously, (when Lalala had gone for a toilet break and I had a brief unsupervised breakdown) and my friend had seen it.

When Lalala got back she immediately deleted the post and made me do the Macarena to show the world how fine I was. But, it had been seen and so it was "out there".

Lalala wanted a night out - she loves a glass or eight of wine with girlfriends.

Another part of me, HOAM (Hang On A Minute) wanted to hide under the duvet and sob uncontrollably.

HOAM is tiny, but she is a constant chatterer. She has sensible glasses attached to a chain around her neck. She is bookish (thin hair in a bun and a neat fringe and has her shirt buttons done all the way up to the top) and she likes to analyse whatever she sees.

Most of the time, Lalala and HOAM get on like sisters. HOAM being the less attractive sister. The one who didn't inherit her mother's cheek bones, but got her dads nose, and in a certain unflattering light, his moustache.

While there is a lot of love, there is also a reasonable amount of shoving and bickering and trying to steal the remote from each other.

HOAM mostly sounds like a mouse with a sore throat trying to be heard over the brass band that is Lalala. But sometimes, very rarely, she can sound as loud as the Red Arrows doing fly-past two feet above your head.

I decided to drive to the meet up place. For me, it was one or The Other. Either drive, drink one glass of wine and have a great evening, or The Other - which is end up at 2.00 a.m. wailing "why doesn't the fucker love me!?" to passing strangers as I stumble down Croydon High Street with an empty bottle of Prosecco in one hand, and my shoes (and possibly my pants) in the other.

HOAM also luckily, has the hard-earned gift of foresight.

My friends were amazing. In fact, the pseudonym of ODFOP was born that night.

I was having a wobbly moment talking about him and my great and wonderful friend Vickstar grabbed my phone and recorded a quick little snippet for me to play when I was having a moment of weakness, to give me strength. It's simple, but effective. It is, in a very posh voice Vickstar saying **"Oh *Do* Fuck Off Philip"**. It works for me like spinach does for Popeye.

The weekend came, and ODFOP and I were still getting on swimmingly. He bought me wine, I cooked him great food. We were happy together.

HOAM by now had pretty much been screaming down a megaphone 24/7 for the entire week. Lalala had wrapped her in clingfilm from head to toe - with a tiny air hole for her to breathe, in which she had put a huge bow made from drinking straws threaded with uncooked pasta stuck together with pink glitter glue.

Sunday morning.

I have thus far failed to mention that ODFOP had moved into the spare bedroom several weeks previously. Initially because he "had a sore back and the other bed was better for him". Then he stayed there because several cats had moved onto his side of our bed and he didn't want to disturb them. Then of course it was because we were no longer together....

So, Sunday morning. HOAM is lying on the floor. Still wrapped in cling film. Snoring the snore of the exhausted and beaten. Pasta and pink glitter stuck to her face and hair.

Lalala had put on a push-up bra and lipstick.

Why not? Me and ODFOP had been like two peas in a pod this last week. He was probably having second thoughts but couldn't bring himself to say it. I was going to have to say it for both of us.

I sat on his bed and asked if we could talk (Lalala is eyes closed, leaning in for a kiss at this point).

He stiffened slightly, and I could feel HOAM waking up....

I took a deep breath and said "what if we were to give it another go? What if we were to use this terrible time as a lesson - a lesson that we got lazy and we nearly lost each other? What if we both make the effort to properly love and cherish each other going forward? I will lose weight and lose my self-consciousness and maybe you can be a bit more understanding about my insecurities and help me get a little more confident? - what do you think?"

ODFOP was silent for maybe 30 seconds. Finally, he said "but we've been here before. I don't make you happy. You hate my rudeness, my Asperger traits" aha! I was ready for this argument!

"Maybe you could work on your Asperger's a little? Maybe you be just a little less blunt and rude? maybe a little more affectionate? maybe saving *US* is worth us **both** putting in some effort?"

Silence, while ODFOP looked fixedly at his computer screen.

I'm hanging here.

He then starts typing something...

I could feel "Fucks sake! can you put down that fucking computer, look at me and talk to me for two fucking minutes you rude ignorant wanker!!" rising from the depths... but I bit it down.

After two full minutes of him typing, he stopped and looked at me and said

"I just don't see our future together. I don't want to try again. I don't love you".

It was at that point that HOAM (who had quietly wriggled her arms free and stood up while Lalala was leaning in, eyes shut, lips puckered for the kiss)

whacked Lalala over the head with a frying pan and knocked her out cold.

"Finally!" she sighed, exhausted but triumphant.

Hang On A Minute was taking over....

III. HOAM Wrecker and a Roar of Unicorns

I had stopped breathing. I was barely able to whisper "ok".

ODFOP started to say something about dinner, while typing on his laptop, but I wasn't listening. I don't think he really was either. I managed to say, "I have to go now" and left his room and walked into mine.

My eyes were stinging, and my insides were being trampled on by elephants. HOAM had Lalala wrapped in cling film and slumped in a chair, still out cold. She wasn't as decorative in her use of crafting material as Lalala, but she was very efficient and robust. Lalala wasn't getting me out of this.

I lay on the bed and just let it all come out. I was basically right back where I started a few weeks earlier, but this time the terror wasn't going to be neatly packaged up and ignored.

Hot Tears and Swirling Void settled in for a solid afternoons work. By early evening, the bin was overflowing with soggy, snotty tissues and I was *exhausted*. I was also **terrified**. Of being over 50 and single again. Of living alone. Of not having someone to call when I was going to be late home from work. Of losing my job and becoming homeless. Of not being able to say, "I'm married". Never being kissed or hugged again. Making wrong decisions and messing my life up. Of being a big, fat, ugly failure with no safety net.

HOAM had been watching this all afternoon. She'd had enough. A very strange thought appeared out of nowhere. Today it's ok to fall apart. It is sad and feeling sad is right and normal. From tomorrow you move forward - no more looking back - there is nothing for you there. Have even just a tiny bit of pride. Taking the easy option is just not an option anymore. Tomorrow you put your Big Girl Pants on and start creating your future, because no one else is going to do it for you.

Curiously, it was just a weeny bit comforting to have a plan of sorts. I slept for 14 hours solid.

On the Monday morning, I started by calling the hairdressers. I've been blonde for the last 30 years. I wanted to go back to mousy brown - I liked that colour. ODFOP liked me blonde - so I had stayed blonde. I booked an appointment for 4.30 p.m. to have my hair cut and coloured.

Taking Care of Me. First Big Tick.

I had no money but decided that a no-going-back-only-moving-forward statement was justified to be put on the credit card.

Learning to be financially sensible was waaaayyyy down on my list of things I could face right now...

I have always been financially irresponsible. Not on purpose of course, but I could never ever summon up any enthusiasm or even vague pleasure in keeping tabs on it or knowing how much of it I had. Don't get me wrong, I am always delighted to be given it. I love a salary increase as much as the next person, but when it comes to monitoring its flow in and out of my life - it is too much of a chore to be bothered with. Like filing, or ironing bed sheets. Stick to a budget? Ha! I say budgetsmudget.

My relationship with money is viewed by my friends and family with a mixture of awe and disgust. For me - you sign your name, or you put a four-digit code into a machine, or you hand over a bit of paper and you get given stuff. Stuff you or friends and family want. How marvellous is that?

And do you know what? When I really need it - it comes to me. Not in giant sacks or anything - but I am never "poor".

Anyhow, here I am digressing. Fully cognisant of my financial failings, ODFOP had worked out what the financial split of the house profit should be when it was sold. I had put in a sizable deposit when we bought the house. ODFOP had not. He had suggested a number and had kindly sent me a "simple spreadsheet" (oxymoron) with how he had worked it out.

On a good day, I would genuinely rather lick a tramps' armpit than open an excel spreadsheet.

The combination of me being safe and warm in Lalala Land and tramp's armpits being widely available - I hadn't opened it. Lalala got to that nugget of information as soon as it came in, and it was now at the bottom of a cliff tapping politely on the lid of its lead-lined box, saying "s'cuse me. anyone there?".

I hear your sharp intake of breath. I know. Luckily for me, even though I don't give a flying fart about money, I am *not* stupid. This was potentially "important money" (another oxymoron), and I had to suit up in the Big Girl Pant's and take control of my financial destiny.

I am also smart enough to know that I am the *worst* person to control my financial destiny. I needed someone who knew about numbers and money and could explain it to me in small words and short sentences. With Lalala still bound and gagged, I had no choice. It was something I had to do. Unless of course I could find a tramp.

I hitched my BGP's up under my armpits and called a financial advisor. He was lovely.

He explained things, so they almost made sense to me. He would take me on as a client. Thank God. Big Tick Number Two.

He needed information to be sent to him. Oh crap. ODFOP held all the financial information. Joint accounts, mortgage payments, bills etc. Never mind. I had, in a rare moment of clarity, told ODFOP that I needed to get someone sensible to look at the money for me. I decided he'd probably be pleased that I was doing something positive about our break up.

"why do you need that? I thought we'd agreed the split?" was his email response to my request for statements. Nervously I wrote back "No, I said I would get someone independent to look at it and he has asked for this information - he is just looking, that's all".

Well, apparently those words were the equivalent of lighting the touch paper and not standing back... Apoplectic is not a word that I have a good use for very often, but it certainly summed up ODFOP's reaction to my response.

I was a snidey, money grabbing, nasty bitch who was "just like my fucking father". The fact that I had engaged a financial advisor apparently "spoke volumes" about my back-stabbing motives. The whole point of "this" was so we could both afford to get somewhere decent to live in.

Oh fartwanktossbollocks! Lalala was still bound and gagged on the chair. I could hear her muffled cries of "it's ok! he's having a bad day at work, it's not about you - he loves you really". HOAM dragged the wriggling chair holding Lalala into the Craft Room and shut the door.

Tears came. Naïve as it may sound, it was only then beginning to dawn on me that this split probably wasn't going to be completely friendly. I still loved him. The thought of him not wanting to ever see me again was unbearable. What if I was wrong? I was blatantly saying that I didn't trust him - how awful am I?

But.... what if his calculation is wrong? what if I am due more of the profit than he says I am? The whole point of "this" isn't about us both getting a decent place to live, it's about us splitting up and each getting a fair amount of the profit according to our individual contributions.

It felt like I could either go with what ODFOP suggested for the financial split and keep him as a friend, or I could challenge him and live in a nightmare atmosphere until the house was sold.

I HATE being in a tense atmosphere. Lalala does her job well. I can forgive, forget, take the blame, apologise repeatedly and generally hop from foot to foot and agree to anything to ease an uncomfortable atmosphere.

35

This was too hard. I needed support and advice.

I needed girlfriends.

Where the inspiration came from I still don't know. It was not something I would *ever* have contemplated. I didn't even think it through (thank goodness). I just grabbed my iPad and I tapped into Facebook Messenger. I looked down my list of friends. Some old, some newish, some close, some were people I had worked for and I'd liked, but our relationship had up until then only been the occasional Facebook "like" or short comment.

I clicked on about 25 names of women whose opinions and life experience I valued, and I messaged them. En Masse.

Most of the them didn't know each other at all. I opened up to them. I said I was going through a shitty break up and I needed support and guidance, and I was asking them for it.

The response was mind blowing.

Ping! Ping! Ping! These beautiful women responded. Every one of them positive, encouraging and full of love. Tears flowed again. But this time I was laughing. Laughing at them introducing themselves to each other and making funny comments about how they knew me. It was **so** much more than I ever could have wished for! I was sobbing with relief and laughing at the same time.

I looked skyward and thanked the universe out loud for these amazing women.

Every single one as rare as a Unicorn, and I have more than 20 of them - all in my corner, cheering me on. How frickin' lucky am I?

Their first task was to advise me on whether to do a blog about my experiences. I knew I needed to see that I was making progress in order to get through this. I had contemplated filling in a diary, but I know myself well enough to know that I would likely give up a diary, or it wouldn't spur me on to make these big decisions and move on with my life.

A blog is public (albeit anonymous). It may even get one or two people reading it. If someone is reading it, I will have to make the changes needed to make a good new life for me. I couldn't have strangers thinking I was a wuss.

They all answered immediately and universally said "Don't be so stupid".

Kidding.

Overwhelming positive responses. ping! ping! ping! Do it! do it!

Gifs started appearing. A dog slapping his owner, a woman drinking tea saying, "we love you", a woman in a metal bra firing bullets from the cups, cats fighting with light-sabres, a herd of unicorns running around...

There was so much interaction with these women who had never even met each other!

Oh, good God! I was late for the hairdressers!

I burst through the door of the very posh and stylish hairdressers - tearstained, no makeup and in clothes that were not really fit to be seen outside of a bin... and with hair that looked like greasy, broken straw. But I was grinning from ear to ear.

Luckily for me, I already had form at this hairdresser. They already had me down as slightly "eccentric", and I'd only been there twice before.

The first time I went there I had blue hair.

I'd put on a blue dress the exact same colour in an attempt to style it out. Dyeing ones' hair bright emerald green, then shocking pink the following week on holiday apparently takes its toll. Back to being sensible and work on the Monday, I bought a hair dye remover on the Saturday. Lots of dye came out - but a huge patch of blue remained... This was the only hairdressers even willing to take a look at my hair that day. They got rid of the blue, and I fell a little in love with them all. Skinny girls with full make up and high heels, all wearing black and looking "groomed".

The second time I went there, I had a small cardboard box with me that contained 3 freshly hatched chicks. I had just collected them and was running late - again. I couldn't leave them in the car in case they got out of the box and ended up under the seats. So, they came in. They sat on my ample bosom while my hair was being washed and made cute "peep peep " noises.

So, they hardly batted an eyelid when I burst in looking like a tramp. I excitedly told my hairdresser all about the Unicorns and read aloud all the hilarious new messages that were coming through on my iPhone. They were very accommodating, bless them.

The next task was to help with a name for the blog. Vickstar came back with "it has to be ohdofuckoffphilip.com" people said it was inspired, they high fived her, another sprayed out her tea across her keyboard. The ideas were coming thick and fast and they were FUNNY!

- Fifty Shades of Chicken Crap
- Bubbles and Break Ups
- Bye Bye Bollockchops - Hello Happiness
- From Henpecked to Happy
- Fleeing the Coop and;
- Chicks, Kitts and Dicks...

In the suggestions there was Bombsite to Bombshell. It was perfect. It described where I am now, and where I wanted to get to.

I would LOVE to be a bombshell. Not the kind that gets dug up in building sites and men run away from obviously, but to be someone that may be of particular interest to someone else. Someone who someone else finds attractive. That would be just wonderful.

I am a long way from that place, but with this blog and the amazing Roar of Unicorns (like Pride of Lions) with me, I know I can get there.

IV. A Potted History of My Life Pre-ODFOP

Please be assured, I don't intend to drag you through the entire history of my life, or the whole gory relationship with ODFOP. Just a few salient bits which I think will give some context to my general state of mind in life - and how I have come to be where I currently am - chained to the bottom of endlessly deep pit of despair and anguish...again.

Actually, as I write this today I am doing decidedly well. It's snowing outside, I have purring kittens either side of me on the sofa, gentle acoustic pop streaming from Amazon Music and I have the house to myself. I haven't even cried for several hours. The box of tissues that is carried with me at all times is sitting there with nothing to do. It's a GOOD day.

So, I'm going to ruin it for myself by dragging up my pre-ODFOP life.

I spent most of my late teens, all of my 20's, and part of my 30's having First Dates. I got *plenty* of first dates. First dates were never the problem. My first date batting average was sky high compared to anyone else I knew.... because they went on to get second and third and fourth dates and even reach the Nirvana that was a boyfriend/girlfriend.

I would do **everything** to be all they could possibly want - all on one date. I would usually insist on paying, AND driving (so they could drink), I would be charming, flirtatious, sexy, coquettish, funny, and furiously nod in agreement to every comment or opinion they had.

The date would nearly always end in sex.

Not good sex either. Selfish sex. A blow job in my car in a car park before I drove them home. Sex at my house, with them getting up and leaving straight afterwards (more than once I would get up and take them home....).

It was not that I was ready for sex, or even wanted it. I was just so *desperate* to be **wanted** by a man.

It was always followed by me never hearing from them again. I would check the phone to see if it was still working - sit and stare at it and check it again. Not go out in case I missed their call. Cry and check it again. Then feel wretched for a month because I was *sure* they were **The One**. What had I done wrong???

But then, 6-8 weeks later, someone would flirt with me, and whether I fancied them or not, I would flirt back, and it was on again. **This** time would be different. This one, really *was* The One. The relief! Oh, thank God!

Friends and even strangers used to joke about my dating history. They used to laugh at me and I didn't even see it. I was too busy laughing too, because well, if they're laughing - it must be funny? Funny is *good*, funny means *loveable*, right?

Inside, I was barely able to function under the crushing weight of the loneliness and belief that there was something dreadfully wrong with me - *but I didn't know what it was.*

I kid you not. I honestly had no idea during all of those terrible, terrible, years **what** I was doing wrong. I wish someone had told me that saying, "the definition of insanity is trying the same thing over and over and expecting a different result". It didn't occur to me.

I was absolutely, certifiably, insane.

I was 31, single, with sixty or so first dates under my belt. All my friends had partners in their lives. I was desperately, desperately lonely.

Fascinated with ancient Egypt, I went on an exceedingly cheap Nile Cruise in the 1996 with a friend...

It was cheap because it was July. *No-one* with any sense goes to Luxor in July.

Perfect for me then.

It was 47 degrees and our flip flops melted on the soft, burning tarmac. Akram was our tour guide on the boat. All the guests loved him. He was handsome, friendly and better than good at his job. There wasn't anything he didn't know about Ancient Egypt. But what made him stand out for me was what he did when the tourists weren't looking.

We (the tourists) were all happily herded from tomb or temple, to coach to tourist shop, stuffing our bags with overpriced tat.

Akram stayed outside. He had conversations with the beggars and the poor who'd flocked to the coach to ask for money.

He always gave the adults money. He gave pens, paper or small toys to the children - wherever we stopped. He'd get the shop owners to give them tea and food to eat.

He was a Coptic Christian in a Muslim land, and he was a good soul. I had never seen such a genuine good male soul in action before. I was astounded by his goodness.

Of course, I tried to sleep with him.

He very gently and very kindly turned me down. I didn't even realise until later that I had been turned down from my horribly aggressive, baboon-bottom-showing "man-attracting" tactic of offering myself on a plate - or without a plate - whichever he preferred.

Like many hundreds of his tour group members before me, he promised to keep in touch and we exchanged addresses.

My friend and I went home and immediately sent him packages of clothes, sweets, pens, paper etc. for the poor people of Luxor.

He did write. Long letters about his family and his life and about funny things that happened on boat trips. Not flirty, just personal and warm. He was funny and articulate, and he was keeping in touch with me for no personal gain.

It was **weird**.

18 months later the massacre at Hatshepsut Temple in Luxor happened. A beautiful monument to a beautiful queen. Terrorists had climbed the mountains behind the monument unseen, each armed with Kalashnikovs'. and had boldly walked up to the temple and just opened fire. They shot practically everyone there.

Akram had been there the day before with his boat load of tourists, and he was further down the Nile when he heard the news. The British Embassy instructed them that all tourists needed to be put on planes home **immediately**.

45

Akram gathered the group of tourists together. They knew nothing. No Twitter or instant social media then. He started by asking them what they thought of the Egyptian people they had met so far. They were all effusive in their positive comments. He asked them to believe that 99.9% of Egyptians were like the ones they had met so far. He then said he had something difficult to tell them.

He'd done his job a bit too well. As a result of his careful explanation, 90% of his boat load of tourists didn't want to go home. They didn't want to abandon the Egyptian people and they trusted Akram. They even made the news. They were practically dragged like protestors from the boat to the airport by the British Embassy staff.

His very hard-earned career was over. Egypt never really recovered from that incident.

So, there we were. One good man (by now good friend) stuck in Egypt with no career. Me, lonely, earning good money, living alone and in need of a good man.

For those of you fellow Minion fans think *Lipstick Taser!!*....**Lightbulb**!

We got married in a registry office in the March 1998. My sister and my parents were witnesses, and we went to Hastings for fish and chips to celebrate.

Of course, we both knew it was never going to work between us.

46

I was older than him, utterly a fruit loop and had no idea how to be with a man beyond the first date. He was an Egyptian man, religious, had never even dated, but had a firm idea of what a wife should be.

We had a fun first year and a following one of not so much fun.

He was working for an airline and doing really well for himself. On a flight from Armenia to London, he met someone far better suited to him. She was beautiful, young, and had a pure innocent heart. Even I couldn't not be happy for this great match of lovely people.

My parents by this time, loved Akram like a son. He moved in with them and he told me to get a lodger.

Enter ODFOP.

He answered an advert which I didn't want to place. Akram knew I shouldn't live by myself and a lodger would be easier than a husband. I was heartbroken, wondering (again) what I was doing wrong - even a patient, kind religious man who loved my family couldn't bear to be with me. Anyway, ODFOP knocked on the door and I reluctantly opened it.

"Oh bollocks" I thought. He looked serious and tight lipped.

There is something you may have already cottoned onto - if you're sharp.

I'm not entirely sure if it was a manufacturing fault, or whether I was dropped on my head as a baby, but my people-pleasing programming has always been stuck at "R" for "Ridiculous".

True story, I was actually asked to leave an "Assertiveness" course when I worked at Coopers & Lybrand.

The trainer said if I was going to insist on finding a way to do everything anyone ever asked of me, whether or not it meant me dying of exhaustion or having no money - and not even be *open* to the fact that it was right and proper for me to say "no" occasionally, he frankly couldn't help me - and I was making everyone else (who was there to learn) feel uncomfortable... I agreed to leave immediately - for god's sake, I wasn't a *monster*, I didn't want anyone else to feel uncomfortable by **me** being there.

It was the first afternoon of a two-day course. I spent rest of the first afternoon in the toilet crying and the entire second day in a toilet cubicle one floor up. Just sitting there on the toilet - seriously wondering "what was so wrong with *helping* people?"

I know. **Now** I know. Back then I had no gauge of scale of balance.

So, miserable lonely people-pleaser opens door to stiff, formal, serious man.

I had no intention of taking a lodger. I had only placed the advert to please Akram. ODFOP had telephoned and told me he was coming to see the room. So, not knowing how to say, "hang on a second" I just agreed -

and here he was. Looking round my house. The house that I mostly sat and sobbed and drank too much wine in.

I thought I would say something like I had others coming to see it and I would let him know. Then I would call and tell him that it had been taken by someone else. easy. He told me he lived in Eastbourne with his wife and son, but he worked in Croydon. He needed somewhere to stay for Tuesday to Thursday only.

I told him some other people had arranged to come around and I would let him know. He said he needed to know now and asked me right out if there was any reason why he *wouldn't* be acceptable to me as a tenant.

He leaned against the oven and looked at me with his arms folded.

Fuck! People-pleaser took over from Pathetic-avoider-of-confrontation and told him that he would be absolutely great, and I would cancel the other applicants immediately.

He then promptly negotiated (as in asked, and I agreed immediately) to a reduced rent as he would be away more than he would be here.

Slam dunk! I had a lodger I didn't want for less money than I was willing to accept.

Still, he was happy so that's what really mattered.

ODFOP moved in to my Loft Room the following week.

V. ODFOP Becomes Lodger ODFOP

So, how can I describe the first few weeks with ODFOP under my roof? I know. Totes Awks. Obvs.

Yep. I think that describes it well. He was already in my home when I got home from work, for a start. I'd become used to my evenings after work following a certain organised, comfortable and completely slobby pattern - and he was disrupting that.

I'd got it down to less than two minutes from entering the front door to me being settled down in front of the telly with wine, for the evening. Now several steps would be, probably, socially unacceptable for a Landlady. Damn it.

Things I could now no longer do between Tuesday and Thursday each week.

- Kick shoes off and leave by door. Ok, I could do that, but I'd probably now have to actually move them, so he didn't break his neck leaving the house in the morning.

- Take bra off under my shirt at the door and toss it on the back of the sofa, usually on top of yesterday's bra.

- Grab face-wipe from packet as I walk to kitchen, vigorously rubbing make up off with one hand and picking up remains of previous night's dinner with the other, on the way through the lounge. Now, I was going to have tidy up after myself - probably *even the night before.*

- Chuck used face-wipe as close as possible to bin... I'd probably have to make sure it was put it in the bin - if he was looking

- Put yesterday's wine glass into dishwasher. Again, probably now I'd have to put it in the dishwasher before I went to bed or some kind of ridiculous bullshit like that.

- Open fridge and choose dinner - would it be Chardonnay or Sauvignon Blanc? - or both? Oh God, I was going to have to buy, prepare and serve proper food.

- Pour first course (which was usually the bottom half a bottle of the previous night's second bottle of dinner) into glass while undoing work trousers and blouse.

- Let trousers fall onto kitchen floor and kick them into pile of other work clothes to go into washing machine at weekend. See what I mean? FFS. Perfectly good evenings, now **ruined**.

- Walk with wine up the stairs while taking blouse off. Chuck blouse in laundry basket - or near laundry basket. I was going to have to do the whole undressing thing in my room with the bloody door shut.

- Step into grubby pyjamas or track suit bottoms, which were ready prepared on the floor from being stepped out of before getting into bed the night before. Grab fluffy, comfy and possibly wine-stained slouchy top off bed and put on. I was going to have to put *clean* clothes on - I'd also have to get new sets of slouchy clothes that didn't have holes in the crotch.

- Come downstairs, go to fridge and get new bottle of dinner and cover with frozen bottle jacket from the freezer.

- Drop down into sullen slouch and click the remote control.

All that was left of my two-minute comfortable routine was feed the cats. Everything else was going to have to become *more acceptable.*

I was very aware that of this had to change because I had been too pathetic to tell a man I didn't know or care about, that the advert was a mistake and I just didn't want a frigging lodger. Inside my resentment glowed like embers in a breeze.

While I was plotting to cut his brakes, I was of course, falling over myself to make him feel welcome.

I cooked great food, I bought him beer and shared my wine. I asked interested but not intrusive questions about him and his life and told him my all about my delightfully perfect and happy one. I even kept my bra and make up on.

It was *exhausting.*

On the Friday of the first week, I came in from work and just fell on the couch and cried. I was so disgusted with myself.

I was pretty sure that "Normal people" didn't let themselves get railroaded into doing things they didn't want to do. Why did I insist on hiring the sodding Orient Express, filling the firebox with coal, buying everyone first class tickets and serving them cocktails on the journey to somewhere that I didn't want to go?

How were every day kinds of people able to *bear* the risk of being unfair/unreasonable/ unkind/thoughtless and *upsetting* someone? How come other people seemed to be confident of their own opinions? I just didn't have the first clue how it was done.

That weekend, hating my every breath, I re-painted his room (I noticed a scuff mark on the wall) and bought new bed linen for him. I shopped and cooked and filled the fridge with things that he mentioned in passing that he liked. Beers, blue cheese (which I could never stomach the smell of) baked beans, and an assortment of other things I would never eat.

Pretty much from the get-go, the four days that he wasn't there, was spent preparing for him to arrive and be as comfortable and welcome as possible, on the three days that he was.

We slowly got to feel more comfortable around each other and got into a routine. Of course, my routine was maniacal, but looked effortless, and his was, well, actually effortless.

On reflection, 17 years later, with so much concentrated experience of ODFOP under my belt, I can see that he was excellent at deflecting questions and changing the subject in a "these are not the droids you're looking for" kind of way. Of course, at the time, I was too busy trying to please this human Cuckoo, that I didn't notice.

As the weeks went on, we got more relaxed with each other. We drank more wine. With more wine, the coat-hanger-in-my-mouth-smile slipped a little. I confessed that I was in fact, heartbroken and my husband was too good for me. To my absolute amazement, he started to open up too. He thought his wife was having an affair while he was working away during the week.

There was no real emotion attached to the words, but I felt his pain *for him*. I had to help him in any way I could. My problems and heartbreak were happily shoved in a box and thrown off a cliff, and I focussed on being his therapist and cheer leader.

He did something that shocked me. He put software on her computer at home and could see what she had been typing while he was away. It felt so *intrusive*, but he was bold and unashamed. He printed them off and brought them home for me to read.

She wasn't having an affair. She was having two or three.

One of my ways of "helping him" was to boost his ego about what a lovely chap he was, while simultaneously describing why I was dreadfully undeserving of the love of a good man. As I think of it now, it makes me cringe. But I was good at it. It didn't come across as me trying to competitively top his problems. Of course, I would never *presume* to think my problems were anywhere near the same level as his, but it was so very carefully crafted to insist he stand on my shoulders to get himself out of this dreadful pit of despair we were both in.

I genuinely did care about him. I cared about anyone with a problem that needed solving.

As the weeks turned into months, we became friends. I opened up a little more about my insecurities and my sub-zero self-esteem.

Once, he got four numbers on the lottery and he bought the wine for the week. I was amazed that he would spend his money on me. Of course, you already know dear reader, that I was spending much more than his rent on keeping him in the manner I insisted he became accustomed to.

Eventually, he could stand no more of his wife's affairs. He informed me he was going to leave her. He asked if he could move in full time for a while. "Oh, fucking fucking fucking hell!" I thought as I smiled and said I absolutely *insisted* that he did.

The following weekend he brought a car load of his stuff and moved it into his room.

As I enthusiastically helped him with his boxes, I was screaming inside "I have absolutely no where, and no time alone to hide - I can't do this!!!"

It was April 2001. Little did I know then, just two weeks later, things were going to get **weird**.

VI. The Thunderstorm of Fate

The first week to 10 days of full time ODFOP were OK, I suppose.

I had to restrict my Unsupervised Meltdowns to the end cubicle in the Ladies toilets at work. It was really quite inconvenient. I am not a pretty crier, so I need to cry alone. I get blotchy and puffy immediately and always get mascara in my eyes which makes them leak even more, and sting. The blotches last for ages. I hate crying at work.

In my job, which is in Human Resources (aka Human Remains, Bloody Personnel, Grim Reaper, Evil HR Lady) I generally get to see a higher than average number of unhappy employees per working day. Some days are great. One way or another I get to help people every day.

Maybe it's helping someone resolve long standing issues that they've had with a fellow colleague that they just didn't know how to resolve.

I get to coach new managers (or just bad managers) on how to approach and manage the more challenging conversations with underperforming members of their team, and I watch their confidence grow.

I get to know and help people who are off on long term sickness and help them access support they didn't even know existed - and then help them gently back in the workplace when they are recovered.

I also get to help people that have got themselves so stuck in a rut in a job that they hate and resent, build the courage to take a leap of faith and look for something they actually want to do all day every day.

These parts of my job are a privilege and they delight me.

The other side of my job is the more challenging side.

Taking people through a redundancy when they're scared of never finding another job.

Working with people who are being bullied and have lost their confidence and have low self-esteem.

Chairing and managing a disciplinary hearing.

Dismissing people who, for whatever reason, just can't do their job well enough.

Being the contact for an employee who has been diagnosed with an illness and they know they're never going to get better, but they still want to talk about coming back to work.

These parts of my job are an even bigger privilege than the easy, happy stuff. If I do it well, I get to make that really shitty, scary time a little less shitty and scary and I watch people transform before my eyes.

People generally are amazing.

Sometimes, very rarely, despite everything, I also get to see that an individual really is an amazing shithead with no redeeming qualities whatsoever.

So, it's all about balance. 99 amazing inspiring everyday people take the same amount of energy as one total dickhead. Such is life.

Anyway, as I said, I've sat across from many an unhappy employee in my time. I've never been afraid of someone crying, but I've always admired people who look like they're going to cry but then they manage to *hold it in*. How does anyone do that? If my eyes tingle that tingle of tears pricking up, my brain sounds an alarm "Here she goes - all hands to the pumps - get those tears flowing and those nostrils filled with runny snot. Come on people, move it! move it!" and there I go. I don't think I have EVER been able to hold tears back post-tingle.

I have only once cried when actually doing my job. I had to make a lovely friend redundant. Her tears and my pain of no longer working with a good friend tipped me over. But apart from that time, it's not my time to cry. This is about them, not me. I always manage to keep the tingle away until they are done and fine and I've calmly walked to the end toilet cubicle.

It is true that people in HR always have a box of tissues handy. Most of the time we use them ourselves, in the last cubicle of the Ladies toilet.

So, where was I? Oh yes, using work time for personal meltdowns. The number of 20-minute sessions of sobs in my designating crying cubicle had gone up over the last week to 10 days. When I am happy with my life, it can happen as little as once a quarter. If I'm heartbroken and lonely and the Lodger has moved in full time, it can get as high as twice a day.

Despite the inconvenience of not being able to meltdown in the privacy of my own home anymore, we were getting on well. He was sad and nervous about starting again, and I was sad and nervous that he was there all the time, but we kept each other chipper.

My niece (Banana) used to come and stay in the spare room periodically at weekends - she'd go to a nightclub nearby and so it was convenient for her to crash at mine. ODFOP had met her before several times and he had no choice but to like her. She is a force of nature. She is bright, funny, and playful and you are swept up in her whirlwind of chatter and happiness. Her granddad's 75th birthday. She quietly and seriously tied several helium balloons to tufts of his hair and beard like it was perfectly normal.... and left him like that all evening.

Well, anyway, Banana had passed her driving test that day. She'd taken her test locally and had come to stay at mine, with her boyfriend, Pistol Pete.

That night there was an AMAZING lightning storm - real horror film action with rain lashing down.

I'd bought her a bottle of champagne and I wanted to give them some alone time - and I really wanted to see this storm. If I'd have gone to watch the storm by myself, ODFOP would never have thought of quietly retiring to his room to give them some time alone, so I asked him to come with me to a place up the road where we could sit in the car and watch the storm over the whole town.

Bemused, he agreed.

It was incredible. Deep purples, greys and flashes of brilliant white lighting up the sky. It was raining so hard the windscreen wipers couldn't keep up. I parked up and we sat there. I was literally clapping my hands together and bouncing in my seat like a child being given a fluffy pet rabbit for Christmas. ODFOP looked like he was watching paint dry - but it didn't dampen my enthusiasm.

"I've got to get out of the car!" I squealed and opened the door. Sideways rain blasted in and I leapt out and slammed the car door. I ran across the road to an open park area that looked down on to most of the town.

I know. Stupid thing to do. But, if I had been struck by lightning I would have died with a big grin on my chops, as it was just the best storm I had ever seen. I was standing there, arms out to my sides, head back, eyes shut, seeing the lightning behind my eyelids, the pounding rain lashing my face and body. I was soaked to the skin, but I felt so alive. I can truly say that was one of my happiest moments, ever - right then.

Then someone came up behind me and put their arms around me. WTF???

ODFOP put his chin on my neck and held me tight. "You're bloody mad. You're going to get killed if you stay out here" he said in my ear.

Let me back up a little here to make something clear. ODFOP and I had shared a house for over a year by now. We had **never** flirted with each other, we had **never** even *touched* each other, even accidentally brushing past each other. We had never, ever entertained a moment's thought about each other in any way that was anything other than friends.

It felt lovely. It felt so romantic. It felt, so right. Without saying a word, we sideways crab-walked to the shelter of a big tree. I KNOW. Stupid thing to do. We stood there, ODFOP behind me, arms round me and me resting my hands on his arms. Neither of us wanted to move for fear of breaking the spell. We must've stood there, not talk ing, just watching the storm and holding on to each other, for about half an hour.

The storm had moved away a few miles and was doing spectacular things in the distance. The rain had softened a little. We had to move. "come on" I said, "let's go and follow it". I drove to another huge open space a few miles away and got out again. ODFOP stayed in the car - possibly common sense had reengaged and he actually didn't want to risk being struck by lightning. We stayed out for about two hours, and when we got back Banana and Pistol had gone to bed. We were soaked through to the skin and dripping on the carpet.

A case of the *Nowthisistotesawks* swept over me. and I quickly said I was going to have a hot shower and go to bed. I raced upstairs, showered and got into bed. WTF just happened??? I didn't know how I felt about it. I loved being hugged - that was a huge tick. Being hugged while watching an amazing storm - massive *humongous* tick. Being hugged by ODFOP? More than a leeeedle bit unexpected and weird. Was it ok? How would we act with each other tomorrow? Oh Gawd.

The next day we managed to avoid each other in the morning getting ready for work. Quite frankly all day I was dreading going home and seeing him. How would we deal with this? It definitely happened. It couldn't be brushed away as he slipped and just grabbed me on his way down. I didn't fancy him. I cared about him. But I just *loved* that long silent hug.

He was home when I got in. Sitting on the sofa watching the television.

"Hi".

"Hi".

"I'll just get changed and then I'll make some dinner" and I raced up the stairs. Oh bollocks. Right, get a grip woman. We lived in the same house, we couldn't be horribly awkward with each other for ever, I'd have to style it out and act like it never happened.

I styled it out and acted like nothing had happened. I made dinner, we sat with our feet up on opposite sofas. We agreed what to watch on the television, we chatted.

Yes, we could do this.

Then something very odd and unexpected happened. I can honestly say there was no thought process involved at all. I was as much, if not *more,* surprised than ODFOP to find myself getting up from my sofa, crossing the lounge and crawling in under his arm on his sofa.

WHAT???? There I was snuggled in between him and the back of the sofa, my head on his chest and his arm round me. I was in shock. He was in shock. How did this happen? We both stayed there, frozen and in shock, but deliciously comfortable and warm, for about two hours.

The end of a programme. No idea what programme. I don't think either of us was paying attention. Right, time to extract yourself and get to bed without looking him in the eye...

I made a move and pretended that I was watching something fascinating on the television which I made a point of remarking upon so we were both looking in that direction. I got up, stretched and said, "night then" and shot upstairs. No idea - again, what just happened.

The following morning was Saturday and ODFOP was going away for the weekend to visit a friend of his. I heard him get up. I didn't move in bed. I heard him go downstairs and faff about. "why isn't he going???" He was making noise downstairs for an *age* - I was dying to go to the toilet, but I couldn't get up until he'd gone, because then I would need to speak to him and I had no idea what to say.

Eventually he went, and I raced to the loo and sat there wondering what on earth was I thinking last night?

VII. THE JOEY TEXT

He'd be gone for all of Saturday and Sunday morning.

Excellent. Time for **me**.

I shopped and cooked and bought myself some (read quite a lot of) nice wine.

It was just so gloriously lovely to be able to just fart and pick my nose without having to get up and go upstairs to the toilet and pray it didn't come out as a loud, raspy one.

Most of a bottle of wine into the evening, I was relaxed and happy. Ping! A text on my phone. It was ODFOP.

"How YOU doin'?"

Bear in mind, these were the days of Friends, and so of course I read it in the style of Joey. It made me smile.

It was also, regrettably, the era of "wassssuuuppp".

"I'm doin' good. Wasssuuuuup?"

"LOL. wondering what you're doing"

"just watching telly and drinking dinner - the usual. What are you up to?"

"Been building a wall with my pal Keith today, but I've been thinking about you"

"Really? I wouldn't have put money on you having brick laying skills. You are clearly a man of hidden and varied talents"

"LOL. So, been talking to Keith about you. I loved you coming and cuddling up with me the other night. I think we should do that every night - what do you think?"

Eeek! half (read three quarters) cut and enjoying the novelty of being flirted with by text, I carried on.

"I loved it too. Honestly have no idea what made me do it, but I am pleased I did"

"me too. what do you think about you and me giving us a go?"

"blimey! I don't know - what if we don't get on and we break up? we're living in the same house, it could be the end of a friendship"

"why would we break up? We know each other well, we get on. What if it WORKED?"

"good point well-made sir. Let's talk about it tomorrow when you're back"

"ok. But I think we should do it"

"that's coming across. :o) see you tomorrow. Sleep tight"

"sweet dreams"

Oh, holy mother of God! Now what do I do??? I read and re-read the texts a dozen times, grinning from ear to ear. This kind of flirty texting had **never** happened to me before. Obvious sex texting that made me feel uncomfortable and a bit grubby, several times, but never innocent *flirty*.

In my mid-teens, my first true love (who lived about 5 houses up the road from me) used to kiss me goodnight, and then go home and write me a letter (Dear young reader (under 30) to answer your questions - yes on paper, yes with a pen - Jeez - no, we haven't always had laptops, tablets and mobiles...). In shiny silver writing. Sometimes it was silver ink with purple outlines.

He, Geoff, was a beautiful writer and I delighted in getting the letter through the door after midnight. I was 15/16 then and that was the last time I had felt cherished by someone who wasn't my mum. We were troubled souls together and I loved him. He broke my heart by falling in love with the girl who moved in across the road.

Ironically, she is one of the people I would jump in front of a bullet for now, and he is someone I would more likely be firing a gun at.

Still, back then I spent a whole year sitting on my bedroom windowsill watching his bedroom window while I sobbed and sniffed and wondered what I had done wrong. Now, 20 years later, someone who actually knew me, was *still interested* - and not just for a fully paid-for night out followed by a shag.

Tiny fireworks were going off in my brain, Lalala and HOAM were crying and hugging, then linking arms and dancing in a circle one way and then the other. There were still very clear niggling doubts though

"you don't fancy him though",

"what if he's a terrible kisser?"

"what if I don't want to kiss him?"

"OMG I *don't* want to kiss him - he's my Lodger for God's sake!"

Confusion reigned, and I took myself off to bed.

I woke earlyish to an overwhelming fight or flight feeling rush over me - OHMYGOD, he was coming home in a matter of hours and I just didn't want to face him because I didn't know what I felt about him. I'll just hide, in my wardrobe, for the rest of my life. Yes! it's a plan - not a great plan, but it's the best I've got for now. I'll stock food in there and a bucket. I'm sure he'll get bored and move out, eventually. Oh, crapping crapsville....

I was sitting in the spare bedroom on the computer when I heard the key in the door. He was much earlier than I expected! A wave of surfing elephants crashed in my stomach. Right, act natural. He seemed to race up the stairs and came straight into the spare room almost out of breath. Acting as naturally as possible, I froze.... staring fixedly at the computer screen.

"Hello!" he said. I wasn't looking, but his voice was smiling. It made me tense even more.

"oh, hello" I said "I'm just on the computer" I mentally face-palmed. It didn't take anyone with super-spidey senses to notice I was not OK.

He left the room and went downstairs. I didn't even turn around. Oh God how rude am I?

My fear of being rude and upsetting someone trumped my fear of someone actually possibly liking me, and so I got up and went downstairs and sat on the other sofa. I looked at him and he looked at me.

"I feel odd" I said

"I see that"

"I'm just so worried that we live together and you're my lodger and we're friends and it's all happened out of the blue neither of us thinking any relationship thoughts about the other up until a few days ago and now it's freaking me out and I don't know what to say or how to act" blurted out at super-speed without me drawing breath.

"Well, I don't have any of those worries. And frankly I have been thinking about you for a while now, but I never thought anything would ever come of it. After last night I couldn't wait to come back - I raced home as soon as I politely could. I couldn't wait to see you"

"Oh"

"I just can't see any way that we could fail. We know each other, we know each other's baggage, we get on really well - why wouldn't we work out?"

"Oh, bloody hell. I don't know!!!!"

"So, why don't we give it a try and see?"

"I can't think of a good reason, except I am scared of losing our friendship"

"we won't lose our friendship, this will be better than just friends - what if we worked really well like I think we will, what if us getting together made us both really happy?"

"Oh well, damn it, when you put it like that it would be stupid to not give it a go - but I want to go slowly."

"of course. We'll go as slow as you like. Right, now let's leave these sofas and meet on the floor in the middle and read the papers together"

So that's what we did. We lay on our stomachs on the floor and read The Sunday Times together. There was part of it that we had done together for the last few Sundays - where there was a section of Birthdays of Famous People. Either he or I would read the name out, and the other would guess how old they were.

Surprisingly, it was great fun and it was something we continued to do for the next 14 or so years.

My head was lying on my hands and he was reading me an article about something and I was loving it. I think I smiled and looked at him. He leaned forward in that "I am going to kiss you now" way and I jerked my head up a little too quickly and nutted him in the mouth.

His lip bled.

He looked so shocked that I snorted a stifled laugh and then a laugh just burst out and I rolled around the floor, tears streaming from my eyes. I had headbutted him!!! He was dabbing his lip and looking at me like I was completely mad, which just made me cry with laughter more, I was literally hysterical...

There was at least 10 minutes of "No, I've finished, I'm fine now... right, no, I've stopped followed by me snorting again. ODFOP I think was a little bemused that I was crying and holding my aching stomach muscles over me headbutting him, and just kept a Mona Lisa kind of smile on his face while he rechecked his lip...By the time I had calmed down all my tension had gone. I hadn't laughed like that for a long time and it felt like a good sign. I gathered my senses, and I leaned in and kissed him.

It was lovely. It was very tender and warm and gentle. Gentle snogs had not been offered to me since I was 16.

We pulled back and looked at each other. "Right" he said "that's got that out of the way - now we know we kiss well together - are you ok with continuing to kiss me?"

"yes" I said in a tiny voice.

We kissed on the floor all afternoon, interspersed with him reading me articles, and us playing guessing games about birthdays. It was a wonderful, wonderful afternoon. I made us something to eat, and we lay together on the same sofa listening to music. I was feeling deeply content.

His shirt was loose over his jeans and I dared to put my hand on his warm stomach. Gently stroking him my hand moved up to his navel where I stuck my finger in up to the knuckle and laughed. I was just feeling his chest with my hand, loving the rise and fall of his chest and his beating heart. My hand moved a tiny bit further, close to his nipple. And brushed something cold and metallic. WTF???

I sat up and looked at him, astonished. He was beaming the biggest beaming grin at me.

"YOU, have got a nipple piercing?!" I shrieked.

"Nope. I've got two".

I immediately straddled his legs and lifted his shirt up. OMG! he had little bars in each nipple!! This was the most shocking thing I could ever have imagined. This man was middle aged by the age of 5. He looked like a quiet and trustworthy salesperson - he most certainly never acted like he had any rebellious qualities at all. Yet he had gone to a tattoo parlour and told the person to pierce both nipples... as expected as a nun taking a vibrator back to Ann Summers because it keeps overheating... I was both impressed and a little in awe.

"anything else pierced?"

"no, not right now"

"did it hurt?"

"Fuck yes. I was in shock and came out in a cold sweat after the first one"

"why did you have the second one done?"

"because I knew I would never go back if I didn't have it done right there and then. I was already in shock and pain - I just assumed the second one wasn't go to make it worse"

"did it make it worse?"

"Jesus Christ on a bike, I thought I was going to throw up all over the guy"

"You are shocking!" I shrieked, deeply impressed.

He then went on to tell me something else shocking. He'd once driven all the way from my house to his home in Eastbourne completely naked. Just for the hell of it! He said he had a few scary moments when lorries over took him and they could see down into his car, and once when he pulled up at traffic lights. OMG, he looked so, well, straight and anonymous, but he was a bit of a rebel!

This was going to be at the very least, an interesting time.

VIII.   I Have Found My ROAR

I interrupt this meander through my past for an important announcement.

I have found my roar. This is a **big** deal for me.

For most normal people, defending themselves with anger is a normal part of life. It may not happen very often, but when they feel that someone has been really unjust toward them, they have the confidence to be angry and *show* it. I, on the other hand, get angry plenty, but am never confident that my anger is fair and objective, and therefore a reasonable and justified reaction to the something or someone that has happened to me.

If I love someone, I am pretty much hard-wired to believe that if I lose my shit defending myself then they will;

- be horrified at how unreasonable, thoughtless and selfish I am and;

- be able to articulate that disgust in a way that shows me that I **am** an unreasonable, thoughtless and selfish shit and;

- be horrified, shocked and disappointed at how I didn't know that what I said was unreasonable, thoughtless and selfish and;

- leave me, and tell everyone on their way out that I am unreasonable, thoughtless and a selfish shit - and finally

- everyone would believe them - because Jesus-Christ-on-a-bike woman it was **obvious**

I have been to see therapists about my people-pleasing and sub-zero self-esteem. I have come to intellectually understand exactly *why* I people-please and think so little of myself to such a dreadfully painful degree, but I cannot seem to change it. When I have expressed my fears about standing up for myself and getting it wrong, every therapist has told me that I will naturally find my balance, and to trust my instincts.

I never have found my balance. I don't think I have those instincts. If I do, I certainly don't bloody trust them, because frankly, what do *I* know?

"Aha!" you may say, "In your job, you have to stand firm all the time! You have to have difficult conversations and bring angry, frightened and sometimes downright rude people to the right outcome as painlessly as possible, and you can't do that without standing strong and not giving in".

Mon petit saucisse, you are absolutely right. At work I can be strong, wise, considered, firm, influential and confident in what I am saying and doing - because it is never *about me*.

Anything about me just gets filed either in

File A - It's good, therefore It's Not True - They're Just Being Nice or;

File B - It's bad - Of Course It's Bloody True - It's Actually Probably Worse Than They Say

People I love who are friends and family are generally 100% wonderful. My Roar of Unicorns for example are, to every woman, amazing, supportive champions of "Team Kate". I am blessed and so very grateful and I would jump in front of a bus to save any one of them.

Them cheering me on is amazing.

But any of them saying anything positive about me is met with squirming uncomfortableness and a desire to run away and hide. Which, I am embarrassed to say, is *so much* of an improvement on how I used to act when receiving anything close to a compliment.

Along with Lalala and HOAM, there is a thick, solid, impenetrable shield which deploys in front of my brain. It has a hair trigger and is set to go off and deflect anything even remotely positive about me that is trying to get into my head and be accepted. Nothing good gets in.

To balance that out nicely, I have an excellent and effective negative feedback magnet. I am pleased to say with years of expensive therapy, I sometimes can recognise now that although this magnet is possibly about equal in power to the earth's gravity (me being the centre of the earth) - not *everything* it pulls in as negative truth is always true. Sometimes. Mostly not.

For many years I thought I was realistic and was just good at spotting things that people said or did and interpreting it into what they *really meant*.

The scene in Pretty Woman where Julia Roberts and Richard Gere are in bed, facing each other and Julia Roberts is telling her story of how she became a hooker. She says a sentence that, when I heard it for the first time hit me like a bolt of lightning. She said "somehow the bad stuff if easier to believe". That was to me like ET getting first contact from his world. A face 100 feet tall had just said what I couldn't conceptualise myself.

So, fair to say my people-pleasing skills are honed and toned, and for the most part are now automatic unconscious responses. I do not have to engage any thought process or effort at all. To try and go **against** these well-worn neural super-highway-sized-pathways of habits I had formed and perfected on the other hand, feels a bit like King Canute facing a tsunami.

Faced with the (unique to me) circumstance of having an actual real un-related adult male that may even actually love me *for who I am* (or what I had shown him of me - which was frankly so much more than anyone else had ever seen) I was not going to bloody well lose that by being a selfish son-of-a-gun.

I may well disagree with his opinions on politics, climate change, taking the life of an animal to make a sandwich filing, and whether people who have been given life sentences without parole should in fact just be given an injection and "put to sleep" in order to save the tax payer millions. I can argue those points with gusto and relish and even get a bit shouty about it if I feel passionate.

However, if he has bellowed at me for not loading the dishwasher correctly for the "50th fucking time", I may be brave enough to say, "Oh for fucks sake, everything gets cleaned in there, does it really matter?" but that will normally be the limit of my push back.

If above-mentioned adult male goes on to verbally connect me loading the dishwasher less precisely than if I were to be building say, the first Space Shuttle, to me being **selfish** because he has to "re-stack it every fucking time" or put the "whole cycle on again" then I am wrong. So very very wrong. I sit there in my puddle of wrongness and feel shame and self-loathing.

God forbid I should push things further and suggest that **he** could be wrong. Say I continued the dishwasher argument and shout that he is just an "anal twat who needs to care about the important things in life instead of stupid shit that's irrelevant". Say I did that.

He would go silent and be in a "mood". I would then be pole vaulting the kitchen-island to hug him and apologise and beg for his forgiveness. He wasn't an anal twat, I was rude and I'm sorry. I know my friend dying a few days ago is no excuse for me being snappy. I was wrong. Can we go back to normal now? I promise I will stack the dishwasher the way you have shown me 100 times before. I am sorry you have had to show me 100 times. I really do try and remember. Sometimes I get distracted by something and just forget. No excuse. Please hug me back.

Yes. Exactly.

During our years together, I did get a bit braver. I did push back a bit more. But ODFOP, with his Asperger traits, and me with my no self-confidence, we got into a dreadful, dreadful cycle of behaviours.

He could hold a grudge/mood/anger for **days** without breaking into a sweat. After half an hour, I would be hopping from foot to foot trying to make everything ok with us, unable to bear him being angry with me. *Anything* to make it all ok again. The pain and the self-doubt and the self-loathing, that I had caused him to get angry with me, was completely all consuming. When would I ever bloody learn??

So, people out there, never mind you shouldn't put a Scorpio and a Leo together. For the sanity and well-being of both parties, **always** put People-Pleasers and those with Asperger traits on **different** tables at your wedding.

So, my roar. Apologies for the long winding road to get here. You will be delighted to know that I have cut out about 2,000 words typed today on the same subject, and reserved those for another time, when you have a huge Gin and Tonic in your hand and have an hour that you don't mind never getting back.

17 years down the line. We have split. I am trying to make everything comfortable for both us, living under the same roof but not being together. I have been cooking, cleaning, oh God that's such a lie - I am crap at cleaning. I have been making *less of a mess*. Chatting amicably with him even though my heart feels like it has been trampled on by his ability to fly into his future without the burden of me dragging him down.

You know about the marriedwomen.co.uk saga and how I reacted to that. He came in on Friday night, and I had been working at home and was in the Office. He was super friendly and chatty, and it was a little odd, but I was pleased he was being nice.

He is part of a Christmas Quiz team. It is not a pub quiz, or even University Challenge type quiz. This is set by people who run mathematical think Tanks for the Government or actually really created the theory of how you weigh a star which to the naked eye, is a tiny white speck in the sky. There are people that have to have these impossible challenges to crack in order to stop them throwing themselves off of bridges, because "what's the point when the world is so predictable and unchallenging". Real life Benedict Cumberbatch/ Sherlock Holmes types. ODFOP would love to be even *acknowledged* in life by such an intellect. In this Quiz, there are no questions - there are just a load of clues on several bits of paper. Pictures of people, a bit of Arabic writing, a squiggle and a row on seemingly unrelated numbers. 200 snapshots of different things that teams look at and find a connection, and eventually find a Tupperware box hidden in a cave in Wales that contains a paperclip and a calculator. And that's it - tada! you've won the hardest "quiz" in the world.

My first husband Akram, of course is of Arabic decent, so ODFOP asked me to ask him what this squiggle of writing meant. ODFOP was *asking me to help him*. This was rarer than hen's teeth, so I duly contacted Akram, asked him, and sent ODFOP the response.

He said he was popping out to take the empty wine bottles to the bottle bank and would pick up some kitten food. Did we need anything else? No, I didn't think so.

The Office is next to the front door. I was still working at 7.00 p.m. and he was loading bottles up in his car. He came in and said "Right, bye then".

That was odd.

At most he would normally say "see you in a bit". He was only going to get kitten food for goodness sake.

8.00 p.m. came and went. I had started on my blog by then and so was engrossed and typing like a mad woman.

9.00 p.m. Where was he? I rang him. Rang out to voicemail. I left a message "where are you? getting a bit worried, ring me"

9.30 p.m. Still not back. Rang again, left another message - "really worried, what's happened?"

9.45 p.m. I WhatsApp and texted him "Where are you? are you ok?". By this time, I was seriously thinking about calling the local hospitals.

10.00 p.m. I get a text "I am fine. do not worry"

WTF does that mean? Has he been kidnapped? is in he in hospital and he just doesn't want me to race down and offer my kidney? (Oh yes dear reader, there is a post coming on that very subject at some point...)

11.00 p.m. still not home. Don't get me wrong. I *knew* what was happening. But gorgeous Lalala was protecting me and it was frankly easier for me to pray he was dying a ditch and being a martyr, than accept that he was clearly on a date.

11.30 p.m. I had drunk nearly two bottles of wine and was struggling to type a straight sentence. It was mostly "hesd a frigginghw wankddd sooo bollocwahekfucj" which I had to delete the following morning.

I staggered to bed and heard him come in at about midnight. I got up and shouted down the stairs, "where the Fuck have you been? You were going out to get fucking cat food?!".

He said quietly that he had been out, and he was fine.

I slurred out so very unattractively "have you been on a fucking DATE?"

"No. I haven't. I just met a friend for a drink" he said. He was saying it instead of shouting it.

As he would say, that **spoke volumes**.

"why the Fuck didn't you tell me? I've been worried that you were in a fucking ditch!" I drunkenly shrieked back. "was this a "friend" that you've met since we've split up?"

"yes". His voice was small. His lack of normal anger at me questioning him on anything he didn't want to share with me shocked even the horribly drunk me - but it gave me a tiny snippet of something hitherto unknown - it was confidence.

"How COULD YOU??? You fucking wanker. You had me worried about you and you were on a fucking date? You complete bastard!"

"it was just a drink. It wasn't a date. I just took the opportunity"

86

Here was me, drunk as a skunk, bellowing down the stairs at him and he was being small and almost, sorry. This NEVER happened.

ODFOP had totally lost all patience with me about two years previously and had never bothered to look for it again. I shouted again that he was a fucking wanker and went into my room.

Maybe a thousand times over the course of our relationship I had quietly catastrophized. He was an hour late home from work meant he was dead in a ditch or had left the country with a size 8 pneumatic-boobed 20-year-old. A thousand times he came home and had a very good reason for being late. My catastrophizing has only ever been about ODFOP or other partner-like relationships. In the rest of my life I am happy, optimistic and thanks to Lalala, completely rose-tinted in my view of the world.

I catastrophized because I didn't *deserve* him, and the world would find a way of taking him away from me.

Now he was dating another woman and so was creating a future without me. Computer says "no". New territory but hurt and pain and outrage carried me through. I didn't sleep all night. How could he do that to me? I had done everything I possibly could do to make this separation as un-drama like and as "normal" as possible for him. I had helped him clear the Dining Room so he could make it in to a separate living room for him. I cooked for him. I cried out of his sight. After he told me didn't love me, I never asked him again about whether he cared about me. I let him have this separation on his terms and never once intruded, even though he knew my heart was breaking and I was feeling so alone. I was going to spend Christmas day with him, so he wasn't alone, when my sister and her family asked me to come and have some FUN at their place.

I was so angry I am quite sure I glowed in the dark of my bedroom.

In the morning, I got up and showered like I was a woman possessed. I was *raging*.

I burst into his bedroom without knocking and went off like a rocket at him. I shouted, I cried, but mostly I shouted. He had to move out as I couldn't and wouldn't stand for it. How dare he disrespect me so much. He tried to use his standard "it's your fault" and "how could you be so selfish" sentences, but my inner Wonder Woman batted them away like badly aimed bullets.

Normally it takes me a week to think of clever retorts to his crushing arguments, and by then of course it's too late. But today, my inner WW was shouting out quips that not only shut his argument down, but also made him look like the shit he was for making that argument in the first place.

ODFOP "You're expecting me to move out now? This close to Christmas? Oh, thanks very much"

Me/WW "you were the fucking bastard that "took the opportunity" to meet someone just before Christmas - it's your fucking fault you're in this fucking position you fucking deadbeat twat!"

Think Batman of the 70's with Pow! Splat! Howzzat!

A tiny bit of me was sitting back watching the scene, eating popcorn thinking "holy shit man, you're atomic!" Meanwhile, deep *deep* inside, many years of supressed anger was pushing through the now broken prison door and was running for it in every direction - amazed that it was ever able to see the light of day again.

My anger was like the opening of the doors on the Black Friday Sales in America. Out Of Control. It felt so frigging cathartic. He was contrite and frankly more than a little scared. He said he would never do it again. He was sorry. He didn't think. Full stop. He really was very sorry for hurting me. He had no idea I would even care.

I got up and walked out.

I went into my bedroom and I messaged my Unicorns. "I've just had a meltdown with ODFOP".

I could hear the cheering from my room. I don't think even they realised the magnitude of the event for me.

The tiny prison cell that had held all my anger for so many years was empty. The door, hanging off its hinges. All the anger had escaped. The tiny sobbing kitten who had been stuck, squashed underneath all that anger or all those years, suddenly had room to grow.

There was a Lion standing in that space and she was ROARING. No fucker was going to mess with her now and come off unscathed.

IX. Potted ODFOP

I shall now try and do the equivalent of that play where they do every Shakespeare play in 30 minutes...

After our first evening snogging on the floor and me discovering his nipple piercings, he sent me a dozen red roses to work.

I panicked.

Nothing like this had ever happened before, *and I still didn't fancy him.* I rang him and told him I wanted to go slower than the slow we were already going. He said fine, as long as we didn't go backwards. Damnit! him and his clever mind games - that was *exactly* what I wanted to do...

Three weeks in, and we had been on a few "dates" which were odd but pleasant and had done a fair amount of snogging. Then a long-time friend Sam, and her daughters came around for a spring barbecue on a warm Friday night.

He was the most *amazing* host.

He got them drinks, he cooked the food, he chatted with her and entertained the kids. My friend was watching him and smiling all evening. At the end of the evening she hugged me the tightest hug and whispered *"finally!* you have someone you deserve. He, my darling girl, is a *keeper"*.

He **had** been *perfect.*

Whenever I was out with Sam, I was generally the *"spare friend"* and the consolation shag. She was tall, as leggy as a baby giraffe, white blonde hair, elfin features, and the most beautiful smile, ever.

And she smiled a lot.

She was the happiest and most content person I had ever known. Growing up she knew she wanted children. She had two beautiful girls and they were her treasure - everything and everyone else was icing on the cake.

Pre-kids, we would walk into the pub and it was like those two guys walking into "The Slaughtered Lamb" in American Werewolf in London, but it went quiet in a *good* way. Men would fall over themselves to casually saunter up and offer to buy her (and sometimes even me too) a drink. She was always lovely to these simpering bankers, property developers, entrepreneur's and generally handsome very eligible men that would've sold both their kidneys for a date with her, but she was never really interested.

I was generally waving a huge sign that said, "when she says No, I will sleep you with you".

As I said, plenty of first dates...

Sam liked proper *rough* boys. I think they were her idea of an Alpha Male, but in reality they tended to be uneducated (not as in not having 'O' levels, but in how to be a normal-acceptable-person-in-society kind of uneducated way), ill tempered, ignorant wankers who would either cheat on her, beat her, steal from her or just lay around her house expecting to be waited upon.

She once, when we were about 17, actually *nearly* ran away with a travelling fair.

He, Dan, (Vey call me Dan vur Man. Hur hur!) ran the Wurlitzer and would focus on our car, spinning us round and round until I was seriously wishing I was spun off the bloody thing. Sam was *squealing* with delight. He had a chipped front tooth, broken nose, big forehead, extraordinarily long arms, home scratched tattoos on his neck, face, and arms, greased back black hair in a quiff, a ripped tight checked shirt and excruciatingly tight dark denim jeans. He looked more than a little like a nightmare Elvis impersonator. He was her absolute *dreamboat*.

Two weeks later he left her (of course) standing in the rain watching his caravan carve up the grass as he wheels spun himself out of her life. Sam was bereft. She had love-bites all over her neck, a bruised face and arms, and, we were to discover some weeks later, pregnant.

She followed the Fair to try and get him to take her with him.

After a week of him shouting at, hitting, snogging, having aggressive fucks with her - and her having to sleep (sobbing) on the floor in the caravan of the family who ran the Ferris Wheel - while he slept with someone else he had picked up on the Wurlitzer, she came home.

More bruises and love-bites and her heart in pieces. She ended up with a beautiful baby and the man who worked in the shoe repair place in the High Street. He too had a chipped tooth, broken nose and a black greasy quiff...

Anyhow, look at me digressing all over the place - I apologise, I shall pick up the pace. Sam had given him the thumbs up regarding ODFOP. I too, that evening had been sitting back and watching him. I too, had been impressed.

Mostly I was impressed that he wanted to touch **me** affectionately in front of *Sam*. Mostly people tried to touch **Sam** affectionately and push *me* out of their way to get to her.

He looked at me with *affection*. He leaned in and kissed **me** as he put a sausage on my plate (not a euphemism), and he stood behind **me** and rubbed **my** shoulders as he chatted and laughed with Sam.

94

As he washed up his barbecuing tools (not a euphemism) I went upstairs and cleaned my teeth. I checked my make-up and gargled with mouthwash.

As I heard him start to come up the stairs I went to the top of the stairs and kneeled down. Heads at same height, I kissed him with a new found burning passion. I took his hands and I pulled him up a few more steps and undid his jeans.

Oh yes, dear reader, there was more sausage to be had... (yes, **now** it's one)

We went into my room and had very passionate, urgent sex. Proper waves-crashing-on-the-seashore kind of sex. In the morning, I woke up and he was looking at me, stroking my hair. He said he'd hardly slept. I felt so touched that he was so excited to finally be sharing my bed and hugged him tightly.

That sentence was something that made my heart sing for years to come when I recalled it. It was many, many years later that he explained to me that he hadn't slept because I was snoring so loudly...

2001 to 2005 were amazing. We laughed, we loved, we *even* shared **expenses**. That was a first. We booked holidays and paid half each! I was amazed and delighted. He bought me flowers every birthday.

Even more importantly, every Valentine's day my bouquet would be the biggest and the best at work. Finally, I **loved** travelling home on the train on 14

February. For the previous 20 years I'd been *bitterly* envious of people who had flowers on Valentine's day.

I just could *never* see a day when I would be the one carrying flowers home. And here I was, smiling and apologising profusely when my bouquet was sticking into some woman's face in the seat next to me who had NO FLOWERS.

I ordered some flowers for myself once, when I was at my most desperately lonely. All day at work, I waited for the call from Reception. Colleagues were called and came back grinning like loons with flowers in their hands.

I waited and waited.

They didn't come.

I got home that night to find the slightly wilted flowers leaning up against my front door. In my stupid (probably drunken) state of ordering them, I had given my home address instead of my work address. What was the fecking point of creating a secret admirer if I get them sent to my home address where no other fecker lived??

To add insult to injury the card that I had created for myself, misspelled my name.

Anyway. We were very happy. We'd talked about getting married. He'd had the whole proposal, engagement ring, party, church, flowers, guests, morning suit, bridesmaids, best man, honeymoon thing.

I'd had the "oh bugger, your career is over. Want to come to the UK and we'll get married, and you start again over here?" thing, followed by me being hungover in a registry office with my parents and my sister, no music and no wedding, followed by fish and chips in Hastings, thing.

We both knew we loved each other, so we decided to **not** get married. We didn't need to. We loved each other, that was enough. We'd both done it before and neither of us wanted the expense or to be the centre of attention, so what was the point right?

Wrong.

I *needed* it.

I *longed* for it.

I desperately, *desperately* wanted to be married to the man I loved - and most of all I wanted a ring on my finger, so I could be part of the *Normal People*.

The Normal People were the people that I'd commute with on the train to London, to work. They would be wearing engagement rings and wedding rings and be reading books or the paper or looking out of the window or even sleeping *and they wouldn't be staring at their rings like* "how fucking lucky am I?".

These Normal People *expected* to be married. The women had been *proposed **to*** for God sake. Some man had nervously coughed up proper money to buy a ring and think about proposing - and they were acting as though everything was just *normal??*

I would literally have *killed* to be one of those people. I was doubly upset that most of them were "normal" looking. How did they get to know someone, who wanted to know *them more and more* and then that other person decided that they wanted to spend the rest of their lives with them?

HOW DID THAT HAPPEN??

Except I was happily agreeing with ODFOP that we didn't need to do it. He didn't want the whole "thing" again, and so I pretended that was the *last* thing I wanted too.

I never wanted the big meringue frock or to be the centre of attention thing, that much was very true. The whole being the centre of attention thing would be hideous.

But I so desperately wanted to be *proposed to* and I desperately wanted to *try on wedding dresses.*

Just the experience of going into the shop and **being the one** to try them on - not sit there and watch a friend transform into a happy bride, like I had been on so many occasions before. In my mind, one of the gushing assistants would ask me "how did he propose?" and I'd giggle and blush and say "oh, it was *so* romantic and *so* unexpected!"

In my mind, I would try on three or four big meringue jobs, look in the mirror, feel like a princess, and then reject them all and buy a simple, but classic frock. I just would have savoured ***every second*** of that experience.

Anyhow, it was eating away at me. I brought it up one morning.

We were reading the Saturday papers in bed, which was *de rigueur* at the time.

"you know what? I DO want to marry you". I really hoped that would be enough.

"Nah" he said turning the page of the Saturday Times "we'd don't want all that fuss. it's just for a bit of paper"

"but, I really do. I don't want a big "do" I just want to get married to **you**. It could be just us and a couple of witnesses - we can wear jeans. I just really want to be your wife"

"Well, I'm not bothered about doing it"

"ok, well if you're not bothered, then we can do it then?"

"no, it's just a faff - we don't need it"

"do you want to be with me for the rest of your life?"

"yes, of course. You know I do"

"well, what's the problem then? It takes less than half an hour and nothing has changed - except for me - everything has changed"

"I just don't want to be bothered with it all"

"well I really, **really** do"

"we agreed! why are you so insistent? it's just a piece of paper for god's sake!" (getting annoyed)

Getting out of bed and starting to cry "well, I don't agree any more. I **want** to be married. It's good for tax purposes as well. If it is just "a piece of paper" then why not indulge me?"

"we just agreed to not bother about it. I don't know why you are getting upset - it's an old-fashioned ritual that I don't agree with - **can we leave it now?**"

Sobbing, pacing "no. I can't. If you loved me, you would give me this. I want it. I need it. why is it so hard to just do this one thing? as you said it's only a bit of fucking paper!"

"Jesus Christ - what is wrong with you? 30 minutes ago, we had great sex, and now it's a massive argument? I don't get you!"

"If you won't do this for me, that means you don't love me enough - then there is no point in us carrying on - I am wasting my time with you when I could be looking for someone who **does** want to marry me" floods of tears, hitched speech, snot, *everywhere.*

"oh, for fucks sake. If it really means **that** much to you - we'll get fucking married! - Jesus Christ!"

That, ladies and gentlemen, was my romantic proposal.

Thank you and goodnight.

X. Planning the Wedding... then Not

After I bullied ODFOP into agreeing to get married we booked the registry office. 3 November 2006. It was a Friday and was about 7 months away.

We, (read I) thought we would sell the house, get somewhere new together that was "ours" and not mine, and then get married. Our house was on the market and we had started looking at new ones.

We, (read I) decided that we did need to have a small celebration after getting married, and it should consist of 6 of our closest friends and our parents and some siblings.

ODFOP has one sister and a mum, his father died when he was teenager. I had two sisters and one brother and mum and dad.

I was only going to invite the brother and my parents.

ODFOP is not a family orientated chap at all. His family didn't laugh very much or do fun things. His father was terribly strict, and, according to ODFOP, ran their home and his children like a dictator.

As they grew up, his sister rebelled and ODFOP withdrew into himself and became sullen.

He learned some "fuck you" tricks that his father didn't notice, which gave him great satisfaction.

A good example of a "fuck you" was that he never called him "dad" or "father". He never called him anything. There was an implicit lack of respect.

He would go on to develop this skill to such an extent that I can remember **every time** he used my name when speaking to me in the 17 years we were together. The instances total fewer than 10. There were no pet names, no alternatives, just an absence.

It was always a thrill for me to hear him talking to someone else and him say "my wife".

In later years he would say to me "what do you want for your birthday" and I would reply "say my name". He would sigh "oh, not that old chestnut" and I would never get it.

A couple of times when he was in a good mood and I'd brought it up, he would say my name and my stomach would flip, and I'd squeal like a 2-year-old "say it again!" and he'd say it again. I could do this a maximum of 4 times before he would say "enough". And that was that. But I savoured those times. I hugged them close to my chest and cherished them all.

103

I know.

At about the time of our splitting up he told me he had just read the book "How to Win Friends and Influence People" and in that book it had said how important it was to use someone's name when speaking to them. He said he was going to try and do that. He never did.

Anyway, the wedding. There was what we thought was a nice hotel near Brands Hatch and we (read I) looked into getting several rooms there. After the ceremony, everyone could go back to the hotel, enjoy a lovely dinner in a private dining room, stay over and all spend the next day together.

I bought all the women £100 of spa vouchers each to use the following day, and ODFOP was going to out with the men shooting (clay pigeon). He was even getting mildly enthused about the event.

Then my mum died.

My mum. My mum was **everyone's** mum. She welcomed every friend us children had into our family, and *everyone* **loved** her, without exception. She was the heart and soul of us.

She had been unwell for the longest time. She had Angina and Diabetes and a whole host of other niggling things that cropped up from time to time. But she had amazing doctors who gave her the right medication and her ailments were being managed. She was deteriorating, but imperceptibly slowly. I think we all got lulled into a false sense of security.

We loved to shop together and since she couldn't walk very far, I would borrow a wheelchair from the shopping centre and we would take off at high speed and have a ball.

Most weekends, we would go to Bluewater. On the way there we would play Garth Brooks or Foreigner and she would sing at the top of her lungs, arms out, head back, belting it out with passion. Oh God, she had a terrible singing voice. Like Eric Morecambe once said, "all the right notes, but not necessarily in the right order".

In her wheelchair, she would indicate that she wanted to go into a shop by sticking her arm out. More than once she caught a man right in his soft tissue area... Once a man actually looked like he'd stopped breathing. We apologised profusely and quickly ducked into the shop, snorting to stifle a snigger.

She would spend. Spend Spend Spend. I am my mother's daughter in this respect, of that there is no doubt.

When my family had a business, she would do some administration and get a weekly brown wage packet with cash in it. She saved these up and gave them to whichever of her children was most in need at the time.

She also would consider that *she still had* that money and hadn't spent it, so she could put it on a credit card... Oh good God, it IS all her fault I am so bad with money!!

Once my father bought her a jewellery box that looked like a treasure chest. He filled it with 200 shiny new £1 coins. The coins remained in the box, and she spent *that* money at least 20 times that **I** know of.

She was extraordinarily generous to everyone. She loved to make people happy and she indulged that pleasure. Wonderful, wonderful woman. Full of life and love.

The weekend before she died, me and ODFOP had driven up to his mothers and were going to formally invite her and his sister to the wedding.

On the way up, we'd had an argument. ODFOP didn't want to give them the details of the wedding yet as his sister was still friends with his ex-wife, who was still periodically stirring up trouble. I said his sister wouldn't tell the ex if we asked her not to. He said she would, and he didn't want them to have the details until much closer to the date.

We argued all the way to Milton Keynes. He wasn't talking to me by the time we got to his mother's house.

ODFOP had no issues at all with being moody in front of other people. It made me *so* uncomfortable. I knew that when we went in, he would be in a foul mood, his mother would wonder what happened and I would be over compensating to make it not awkward for her.

She didn't see him very often as it was, and loved him so much, she'd be gutted that his visit was ruined by him sulking.

So, I decided it was better for me to just go home. I told him. He got out of the car and slammed the door.

I cried (of course) all the way home.

We were supposed to be staying there the night and so ODFOP wasn't going to be coming home. By the time I arrived home I was panicking that I had pushed it too far and that he hated me. I called him. He didn't pick up. I called him again. He'd switched his phone off. Oh fuck. I've really done it now. I sent a text and got no reply.

The original plan had been that I would come home the following morning with ODFOP, drop him off and then go and then take mum shopping.

I rang mum and said that I couldn't go shopping as I needed to wait for ODFOP to come home. Normally she was happy to reschedule shopping if I needed to, but this time she said "oh please. Just a little shop?". I said I couldn't as I really really needed to be home for when he came home.

I felt terrible. My mum never pleaded, and I hardly ever cancelled a shopping trip - it was the only time she got out of the house and away from dad.

ODFOP came home on the Sunday morning and I hopped from foot to foot around him to try and make everything ok. It was fine. I was so relieved. He told me that I "go off the deep end" and I needed to "stop trying to control him and his family".

I was shocked that I had got it so wrong and looked like I was trying to control his family, but if he said that's what I was doing, then it must come across like that. From then on, I never said a word about them. I stopped saying "it's about time we go up and see your mother".

So, he didn't. For the next maybe 2 years. She lives less than 100 miles from us.

Anyway, I rang mum the following day when I was at work to apologise and see how she was. I rang her every day anyway. Dad answered the phone. "What's wrong?"

"your mothers not well"

"have you called the doctor?"

"yes, but she can't get there. She says her legs aren't working"

I heard a noise in the background. "What was that?"

"That's your mother, crying". My mum never cried. She never complained. She never made a fuss.

"I'm on my way" I put the phone down and grabbed my things. I told my boss I was going home as my mum was unwell. I got that *look* from her but didn't bother stopping to justify myself.

I had done this before, several times. Mum would be unwell, and the doctor would suggest she needed to go into hospital for a few days. My father was rubbish at this kind of stuff. He'd pack the wrong things, he wouldn't comfort mum, he would just be driven by the process and miss all the **important** bits.

She would generally be out in a few days and all would be well again.

At the hospital there was a lot of people coming in and out. Trying to find a vein, trying to put a catheter in, putting the sticker pads on to do an ECG. This was normal stuff.

I tried to distract mum by talking about the plans for the wedding. I was holding her hand and distractedly tickling her palm doing "round and round the garden, like a teddy bear" like she had done to me and my siblings 1,000 times before when we were kids. She had a dry mouth, so I went to try and find some boiled sweets. Dad just sat on the seat by the bed and tried not get in the way.

When I got back mum was pale and on oxygen. She'd had an oxygen mask before, so Lalala just assumed it was all fine. I gave her a boiled sweet, held her hand and stroked her hair. Over the years, I'd done this 10-12 times. We just needed to get her on to a ward and settled. I told dad to get off his arse and come and hold her hand as well.

The ER doctor asked if he could just have a quick word with us. We followed him into the corridor. He said that he was struggling to find a ward that would take her because there were so many different things going wrong.

We listened and waited for the "but I've managed to find....." followed by the ward that she would go into.

He didn't say that. He said that we maybe needed to think about the fact that she may not get better.

Nope.

We've been here and done this so many times before, we know how it goes - there was an established pattern and the next thing is she is moved to a ward.

He saw the blank look on our faces and said he would continue to try and find somewhere for her.

Right. Excellent. You just get on with that then. We walked back to mum. She was as white as a sheet and looked asleep. Poor mum, she must be exhausted.

I held her hand and she was a little clammy.

I looked at her face carefully.

She wasn't breathing.

I shouted, "we need a doctor here **now**!" at the top of my voice, making my father jump. A few people rushed in, including the ER Consultant. "She's not breathing!" I shrieked.

The Consultant said the strangest thing - he said, "are you sure you want us to try?"

"YES" dad and I shouted in unison.

We were shuffled out and the curtain was pulled round. We sat outside and just looked at each other, dumbstruck. How did it come to this? This wasn't how it was supposed to go. She was supposed to get settled in a ward and come home in a few days.

After no time at all, the Consultant came out of the cubicle and just looked at us both. Rabbits in headlights. He said he was sorry and a nurse would come and talk to us about what happened next.

Autopilot. Dad stayed with mum and I got taken off to a horrible little room that had leaflets in it about "what to do when someone dies". The nurse handed me a couple of leaflets and was talking, but I wasn't listening. I was like a badly tuned television, occasionally coming back into focus and hearing a word and then going static again and just hearing white noise. It was about 8.00 p.m. We left the hospital and I was fighting the urge to take mum's bag of toiletries back to her - she would need them. I didn't really understand why the nurse had given them to me.

I phoned ODFOP and told him. I said I was staying at mum and dads that night. I sat in the lounge listening to dad pace up and down while he called all my siblings. I had lived in fear of getting that call. I couldn't imagine how awful it was to be on the other end of that phone.

I slept on mum's side of the bed next to dad.

Two days later our house sold.

I never went back to our home to sleep after that. My dad needed me.

XI.   The Wedding was on... then off... then on

Mum had died about 10 days before ODFOP's 39th birthday.

I had been **so** excited about planning something big for his 40th birthday, that I had to do it on his 39th. I couldn't wait.

ODFOP travelled a little for work and in those blossoming first years of our love, I had gone with him on several trips.

Geneva was a favourite regular place to visit. There was a restaurant called Café du Centre in the town and they did the most incredible stacked platters of Fruits de Mer that we had ever seen. Stacked high with oysters, periwinkles, whelks, prawns, crabs etc. All on plates of crushed ice.

I could just about pick at a prawn but the rest of it was a huge no-no for me. yuck. But for ODFOP, it was paradise. It could take hours to get through it all, but I have rarely seen him happier than with a long pin in his hand, winkling out a winkle at the Café du Centre.

It was his favourite restaurant in the world.

So, for his birthday, I had got us, and our two favourite friends booked on an EasyJet flight and into a nice little hotel in Geneva for the weekend at the end of May.

Except now my mum had died and I couldn't leave my dad alone in the house. I hadn't spent a night with ODFOP since the day before mum died, and I *really* wanted some time with him.

My siblings were amazing. I couldn't fathom going off on a jolly to Geneva as being anything to be considered when thinking about my mum and dad and the funeral.

They pretty much insisted that I go. Dad would be looked after. Go.

Her funeral was the day before we went. Our friends came.

I was reading out my eulogy to the friends and family there - about our shopping expeditions and mum's sharp left-hand turns, about how she was a mum to every one of our friends, and about just how bloody wonderful she was. I looked over and noticed that ODFOP was crying. Not a solitary tear, but a body shaking, uncontrolled, anguished cry.

I managed to finish, and the next person got up to speak. I sat back down next to him. My poor man. So stoic in so many ways, but full of pain. God how I desperately wanted to take his pain away.

Our friends (the same oh-fuck-they're-coming-for-dinner-tomorrow-night friends as it happens) stayed over with us and we got drunk and talked about mum.

The next day we flew to Geneva. It was beautifully warm, and it was so lovely to be there with good friends that hadn't been before.

That night, we went to the restaurant and ODFOP ordered the huge platter of seafood. I had pre-ordered a cake for his birthday and they came out and sung happy birthday to him which mortified him. We had a great night.

We spent the following day on the boat trip round part of Lake Geneva and sat in the sun and drank lots of wine. It was a beautiful, perfect day.

Two nights in a hotel with ODFOP and friends I loved, and then I returned to my parents' house. I was miserable being away from him.

Our house had sold, and we were due to exchange. Dad was alone and didn't know how to be alone.

The three of us had a big conversation and we agreed that ODFOP and I would buy my parents' house and move in with dad.

I didn't want to. I wanted something that was new to *both* of us.

I didn't want to live in my childhood home without my mum there, but I didn't know how to **not** insist on taking care of dad.

So, we just did it.

There was lots of work that needed doing in the house and garden and it was busy. Dad and ODFOP got on well. The evenings were spent drinking wine, watching telly and talking.

Weekends, ODFOP and I spent in the garden, converting the back half of it to an allotment where we tried to grow all sorts of things.

Sunday evenings in the summer, we would sit in the huge Jacuzzi bath and look out over the garden, sharing a bottle of champagne.

I loved Sunday evenings.

We had cancelled the wedding when mum died. I couldn't think about it. But one perfect Sunday evening, sitting in the bath, legs entwined and bubbles up to our ears, I suggested we re-instate our wedding.

He agreed immediately which delighted me. But this time it would be smaller. Just our best friends (Geneva/oh fuck friends) and I suppose we would have to invite my father, as he lived with us.

We couldn't really say we were just popping out to get married. That would probably be a bit rude.

So ODFOP re-booked 3 November 2006 and we booked the hotel for us and our friends for the weekend.

We talked about rings. Well my lovely one reader, I could write several posts just about bloody wedding rings, but I shall give you the short version - because I like you and I'm grateful you're still reading.

ODFOP wanted a wooden wedding ring. Yes really.

He found someone who made wedding rings from the trees that were torn down to make way for Newbury by-pass. Protestors had moved in to the branches of the trees to stop them from being ripped out. It was regularly on the news in ten years earlier.

ODFOP had no special links with the Newbury protestors, that I was aware of anyway, but he wanted a wooden wedding ring. So, I bought him one. It was beautiful. Made up of tiny pieces of different woods all tightly glued together.

I asked for a normal gold one please. I was told to find the one I wanted and send him a link, so he could buy it.

Wedding rings sorted - for the moment.

Next was outfits.

I was more than a bit overweight, so shopping for clothes hadn't been fun for a long time. Finding something that I looked nice enough to get married in - that was going to be hard.

Cue girlfriends to Selfridges. I hated the shopping bit. I couldn't find anything and got upset so we went to a pub behind Selfridges and drank lots of wine. That was much better.

I ended up with a pair of cream linen trousers, a gorgeous fake fur cream jacket and a top that I hated. But it matched. I bought ODFOP the most wonderful green paisley patterned shirt from Liberty's.

We were all set to go.

I suggest at this point you stop reading and go and get yourself a stiff drink. Or two.

The day arrived. Our friends were meeting us at the registry office (they lived the other side of London). I was curling my hair and trying to make myself like the top I was going to wear. It was 10.00 a.m. We were getting married at 11.00 a.m.

ODFOP's mobile rang. It was our friends. They had got themselves there super early to make sure they weren't late.

People attending wedding ceremonies were permitted to park in the special car park.

They had driven up to the gate and the security guard had come to the driver's side.

"Can I help you?"

"Yes, we're a bit early, but we're here for a wedding at 11.00 a.m."

"I don't think you are sir. There are no weddings scheduled to take place today"

"um. It's definitely today. At 11.00 a.m. can you just go and check?"

"I have been informed that there are definitely no weddings today Sir"

"hang on a minute. Let me just call our friends"

Philip handed me the phone and said he wasn't sure what they were talking about and could I deal with it.

It was my lovely friend. Terrified. "Um, well the security guard says there are no weddings today" she said in a tiny voice, wanting to be anywhere but on the phone telling me that my wedding wasn't happening...

It was 10.15 a.m.

I got on the phone to the right department and they confirmed that there were no weddings booked in for today.

In fact, the Registrar was on a day off.

I went hot. then cold. then slightly screamy.

ODFOP does **not** like it when I get emotional. He copes with it by getting angry with me. Yes, that usually helps.

This wasn't turning into the day I had dreamt about.

He found the email on his phone that confirmed to him that the wedding date was reconfirmed as 3 November and shoved it under my nose.

I told them I was staring at an email that confirmed that we were getting married in about 35 minutes time.

They didn't have that email.

The registrar was on a day's leave today.

My makeup had started to run. ODFOP was pacing, tight-lipped, angry.

"Ooooh, here it is!" said the girl on the other end of the phone. "Yes, he did book it back in. We just didn't transfer it to the booking system. The registrar is on a day's holiday today".

It was like she was talking about a dental check-up and not my hard-fought for, desperately wanted wedding.

It was all going horribly wrong.

"Can you get on the phone to the registrar and ask him or her to come in please? This is something that we were actually quite looking forward to" I said in a sing-song lost-the-plot kind of way. One of my eyes was twitching.

"Oh. I could try. But she is on a day's hol....."

"Yes. You've said. But we've actually put some plans in place around this happening, like a honeymoon (we hadn't but we *could* have). It is *your* error and we are due to get married in less than half an hour. Please call her now and I will hold"

I joked with ODFOP that we would laugh about this one day. I didn't mean it. I wanted to pull my hair out and rip this fucking ugly top off me and get into bed and never get out again.

"Yes, she says she's terribly sorry. She will come in. Can we reschedule for 12?"

"Yes, we can do that. thank you."

When we got there, ODFOP was still in a bad mood.

I wanted to scream "it's our wedding daaaaaaaay!! for fucks sake make an effort you selfish bastard - snap out of your mood!!!" but if I had of done that, well, it would've been so much worse than it was. And it was already quite bad.

Our friends were nervously looking at us like they didn't know whether to laugh, cry, or run away. I suspected my Best Mates Husband was thinking "is it too early to make a joke out of this?" - he looks at ODFOP's sulky face and my barely holding-on face, and concludes" Yes, probably".

Still, big warm hugs from lovely friends, and we both calmed down.

We went straight in and got on with it.

The Registrar was in jeans and it looked like she hadn't washed her hair. She had clearly been having a slobby day off and had not changed before coming in. I was so upset that she hadn't made any effort at all.

Right, fuck it all, **this** is the important bit - the vows, the rest of it is just bum-fluffery. Focus, you are getting married, right here, right now - **remember this moment.**

I cried as I said my vows. I really wanted him to look at me with love and say those words to me. My heart was bursting, *willing* him to do that for **me**.

But he didn't.

He laughed nervously as he held my hands, but he looked at the Registrar as he repeated the words she spoke, and then at our friends.

Within seconds the scruffy Registrar said we were man and wife and that was it. Done. A quick signing of the register and we were out - probably less than 10 minutes - certainly less than 15.

ODFOP and my BMH (best mates husband) had a small competitive thing going on between them. As individuals, their thirst for knowledge is unquenchable. On every topic. The competitive bit was that they *always* had to know **more** facts than the other one on any given subject. BMH had a thing for architecture. He had looked up the details of the building where we got married and knew that it had some interesting cornices (or some sort of shit like that - possibly drainpipes for all I know) on one side. Unbeknownst to me, ODFOP, knowing that BMH liked architecture, had *also* looked up details about the building. He had *printed off* information about it.

We walked out in to the fresh air. Right, time for some pictures?

Nope.

ODFOP immediately started talking to BMH about the architecture and they both went off in search of said cornices/drainpipes. BMH was following ODFOP but looking behind at me and his wife, shrugging his shoulders apologetically.

They were gone about 15 minutes. I think BMH pulled ODFOP back.

We walked to a place to take pictures. ODFOP walking with BMH talking architecture, and me, best friend, my brother and dad following behind, all of us embarrassed about the huge massive elephant-in-the-wedding that was ODFOP's behaviour.

He stood with me for one photo and then took the camera off my brother and told him and my dad to stand with me.

Inside I was screaming - but what could I do? Lose my shit with him on our wedding day? Not a good start. Plus, expressing anger at ODFOP only **ever** resulted in him sulking *for days*. I'd only have to beg for forgiveness and work 10 times as hard as it already was, to make the atmosphere bearable for our friends.

The best I could do was bite my lip and act like I hadn't noticed. But, this aching swell of wretched sorrow, *deep* embarrassment, self-pity and loathing was growing like a repugnant swamp beast. It loomed over me.

I had so, so badly wanted a *nice* memorable wedding day, not a hideous memorable one.

Most people have lovely wedding days, and they have *huge* grand affairs where *so much* could go wrong. This was a registry office with two friends being witnesses and a weekend in a hotel that was 10 miles away. I stupidly thought it was fool-proof.

How had I been so stupid to think that I could have that? *Other* people get fairy tales. Frankly, I got what I deserved. I had set myself up for a fall, and I had roped my lovely friends into this squirming, farce of a wedding day.

We left my brother and dad and went to the hotel. Things could only improve now, couldn't they?

We dumped our cases in our rooms and met downstairs for some champagne in the bar. We sat on some comfy sofas and settled in. The barman came over, took our order without looking at any of us and wandered back to the bar. He came back with the champagne and four glasses. No ice bucket.

"Can we have an ice bucket please?"

"they're all being used" - he said over his shoulder as he strolled casually back to the bar.

I got up and wandered, as casually as I could, over to the bar "We need an ice bucket. Can you please go and find one? We have just got married"

No eye contact, no congratulations, but there was an audible tut as he slouched off.

"I'm sorry. Did you just **tut**?" slight twitch to my left eye.

I casually walked back to the sofas. My Best Mate was looking at me very closely, wondering if I might just go off at any second.

By the time the barman came back, we had drunk the champagne. He just put the bucket on the table and walked off. It was *sans* ice.

By now I needed to give my friends a break from wondering what could possibly happen next, so to lighten the mood I said I wanted some married sex and could we go to our room and meet lovely friends later for dinner?

Relieved, they ran-walked to their room.

I had booked us the honeymoon suite. We hadn't looked at it before now but now we were in it, it was a bit of a tired shithole.

There was pink silly string all over the four-poster bed. The duvet cover wasn't clean. The pillows underneath the covers were terribly stained. The bathroom had pubic hairs in the shower and the mirror was smeared. I was past wanting to cry.

At least we had sex. That was normal for a wedding day? Post-coital, ODFOP tried to put the telly on. There were no batteries in the remote control.

I rung down to Reception and very very calmly asked for someone to bring up some batteries. We quickly got dressed so they wouldn't be embarrassed when they came with them.

They didn't come.

I think by this time my brain was worried about me.

There were two options. I was either going to

1. run around the hotel screaming and stabbing people in a Shining kind of way, or;
2. go to sleep.

I went to sleep.

I woke in time for dinner. Two hours sleep had taken the edge off my desire to murder everyone and I was looking forward to dinner.

Dinner was excellent. ODFOP ordered the most expensive wine on the list and we had a great time. The hotel was so totally and utterly shit at being a hotel, that they failed to charge us for it. Excellent.

We noticed the place was full of groups of women, mostly in towelling robes. At dinner. The Daily Mail had run a thing where you could get 2 for 1 deals at a load of spas, and this was one of the hotels and this was one of those weekends. Great.

BM and I are experienced spa stayers. We know about slouching round all day in your dressing gown and drinking an awful lot of wine. That's where all the ice buckets had gone.

The following day me and BM spent the day in the spa. I had so many bloody vouchers that we had pretty much one of everything they did and got a box of Espa goodies too.

Things were turning around. Finally.

That evening we were going to Leeds Castle to see the firework display.

Now the four of us, many years earlier, had gone to an outdoor classical concert at Leeds Castle and it had been *amazing*. People sat on rugs and had picnics and it was gloriously civilised and lovely.

We thought it would be the same for the fireworks. We had even taken a bottle of Laurent Perrier pink champagne to sip while we watched the colourful display.

Oh nononononono.

It was packed full of people. Jam packed. Everyone behind a big rope. Kids treading on your feet, a loud fun fair, a Wurlitzer controller on a terrible microphone shouting "screamifyouwannagofasterrrrrr!!" Bright lights, big hemmed in crowds, kids shrieking, being pushed and jostled.

If you know anything about Asperger's, you know this scenario was all nine levels of Dante's inferno at once for ODFOP. He lost the plot. Lalala has taken such good care of me, that I can't even remember if we stayed for the fireworks.

Back to the hotel, the men wanted Guinness. The miserable barman said they'd run out of Guinness. They hadn't. We'd seen it in the spa bar earlier that day. We made him go and get it. He wasn't very unhappy with us. The result of their unhappiness was them putting random items on our bill. Nothing that resembled what we had actually drunk.

It took an age to sort out. I was furious. ODFOP and our friends stayed in the bar, knowing that's where they were safest, as I sorted it out and begrudgingly paid.

If I am to be as totally honest in this blog as I said I would be, I am so angry with myself for trying to make that day happen, let alone *special*.

My NEED to be married was so overwhelming, that I dragged an unwilling man and two innocent friends, that I loved, into my carefully crafted play which was designed **entirely** to make me feel like I could join the club of **the normal people**.

Wanting something so badly, does not mean you can, or should have it.

The *real* world doesn't put up with bullshit like that.

I had created a huge, stinking mess, and I was covering it in glitter and telling the world it was a diamond.

Stupid *stupid* me.

XII. My Terrorising "Kindness"

Since as long as I can remember I have been a people-pleaser.

It manifests itself in several ways, and it has evolved, over the years. Different people have different experiences of me, but for the most part there is a thick seam of consistency running through my interactions with people I care about, and even those that I don't.

These days, mostly my people-pleasing fixes are got through money. I think my lack of interest in it makes it easy for me to generally "get my fix". It used to be sex, when I was younger and more attractive.

Now I am large, and older, and have a better paid job, I have a proclivity for largesse.

I would add that I do like to make people happy in normal and non-monetary ways too, but money is definitely my drug of choice for the over-the-top jobbies.

Ninety-nine times out of a 100, I will **insist** on paying for everything.

For any friends out there, that are reading this and thinking - "well, she didn't bloody pay for drinks last time we were out" - I am a work in progress. Sometimes now I can accept splitting the bill if I know people are getting hacked off with me, or possibly sometimes I can allow someone else to pay. It's still a horrible, wracked-with-guilt experience for me, but I am working on being better at it.

And I will get the drinks next time, you can count on that.

I know (now) where the people-pleasing comes from. Thousands of pounds of therapy have dug those boxes up from the bottom of the cliff. They've had the seals broken and the lids opened to reveal squirming, horrible, ugly memories covered in sticky tape, glitter and bows made out of pipe cleaners.

That may be a topic for another blog, one day.

But even though I know it is not rational or realistic, if I drill down and down into the depths of my core values and beliefs, and am totally honest with myself, I am 110% confident in the fact that everyone else on the planet *deserves* to have good things happen to them and I simply *do not.*

Good things do happen to me though. Quite a lot. I count myself as amongst the luckiest of all the people I know. My brother is constantly gobsmacked by the amount of times I can get knocked down to get back up and step into some better situation. I'm *known* for it.

Never with men though, just thought I'd add that clause in, not that I needed to be explicit on that point...

I am incredibly lucky. But I am *not* **deserving**. Different thing **entirely**.

I don't hate myself, don't get me wrong. I have been known to totally pamper myself at a spa, I have got myself a decent car, I eat popcorn whenever the opportunity presents itself (if there is a God, she invented popcorn), and I have indulged my love of furred and feathered animals.

Also, I don't bow and scrape to everyone on the planet. I carry a healthy amount of road rage around in the car and can quite happily call someone I've never met a total wanker for simply not indicating. I don't like selfish people and I can let them know it. I don't think you've got a strong enough stomach to read what I think should happen anyone who purposefully hurts an animal.

What I am trying to say is, I don't think I am meek and mild about it. I *really hope* I'm not pathetic about it. I have plenty of happy times in my life.

I don't know when it happened, when the belief that I didn't deserve good things to happen to me snuck in past Reason and Reality into my subconscious and locked the door behind it. I can't ever remember **not** knowing that it was fact.

With that belief comes the whole scales of balance issue - good things for **you** 50% - good things for **me** 50%. Normal balance of a normal life. Somewhere along the line, the 50% good for **me** was neatly superglued to the 50% good things for **you** weight. So, it's less of a balance and more of just one big weight on the ground.

I am undeserving = everyone else **is so** deserving. Brain says, Post Hoc Ergo Propter Hoc, Clarice.

Most of the time, believe it or not, it is a complete joy to be me, and I don't think I generally offend people. Not every day anyway. I absolutely *love* making people happy - but who doesn't, right?

But, here is a small selection of some of the things I have done in the rock-solid belief of largesse was appropriate and right. I do not wear this list as a badge of honour. This list is an example of how "is it my round now?" isn't what I am talking about when it comes to my determination to **make people happy.**

If any friends are reading this and they see something I have done with them in here, please don't think for one second that I didn't love every second of doing what I did. I don't care about money. If I can do something nice with my money and it makes someone happy, what **I** get out of the exchange is sooooo much better (for me) than what you get. If it made you

133

happy, then huge tick for me. But if you felt awkward, embarrassed or uncomfortable, this is to say I recognise that now and I apologise - you are not alone in me overwhelming you.

- A random man approached me as I left my work on Christmas eve. He was crying. He had no money for his family. He asked for £5. I hailed a cab and we both went to the cash point where I drew out £250 and gave it to him. That was in the 90's when £250 was worth something...

- I wasn't able to make it to a friend's birthday party, so I took her to Marrakesh for a spa break. She tried to pay for some things and I INSISTED on paying for everything. It was a shitty hotel, which made me want to take her again...

- Got 2 suites in Hotel du Vin in Brighton for the weekend (ODFOP's birthday). Complained that there was scaffolding up and got some cash back. INSISTED that the friends took the cash.

- A friend, first time in the UK. Took £500 cash out and just blew it on a fun day in London. That was more money that she earned in 3 months. She was uncomfortable.

- Someone said they liked my sapphire ring, so I gave it to them and INSISTED they keep it

- Bought a 5-star all-inclusive holiday for a friend and her boyfriend, because they didn't have enough money to go on holiday and she happened to mention it to me. They would never in a million years have booked a 5-star hotel themselves. They felt out of place and intimidated.

- Pretended that I had got a free business class flight to Los Angeles to take a friend. She had, just in passing wistfully said that she didn't think she would ever be able to afford to go to America, and certainly never be in Business Class

- Took the whole team of people I worked with for Tea at The Ritz because someone mentioned they'd heard it was lovely there. Someone suggested we should split the bill and I made a bit of a scene trying to get the bill off them.

- Spa break with 5 friends. Popped out and paid the bill while everyone was finishing breakfast. More than one of them was a bit horrified.

- Sold a car and had £1,000 cash. A friend (who had a good job and earned more money than I did) mentioned how he was broke so I gave it to him. He was mortified but I INSISTED.

- A friend was having to save up to have her car mended. Getting to work was a pain. I offered to give her the money. She vehemently refused. I posted it through her door and didn't answer her calls until I saw her car was working

- A friend fancied the chap I really liked (and was trying to attract by sleeping with him). I'd bought tickets for me and him to go to a Meatloaf concert.

I gave her my ticket, booked a nice restaurant for them before the concert, rang the restaurant and paid the bill. They went out with each other for 6 months and it broke my heart.

- Paid a friend's mortgage and her mobile phone bill for 4 months while she was out of work. Refused her attempts to pay any of it back.

- A friend who'd been on a round the world trip with her family came back and was a bit broke. Gave her £2,500 and INSISTED she keep it. She asked to borrow another £7,500 and I gave it to her, even though ODFOP was screaming at me not to.

- Two nights in a spa with two other friends. They'd never done the spa thing before and I tried to make them have expensive treatments. They tried to split the bill. I actually cried until they let me pay.

I have practically wrestled friends for the bill at restaurants - beyond polite insistence, when they have really wanted to pay for it, or split the bill. This actually is most people I know.

I have taken their cash and thrown it on the floor, so they are distracted and have to pick it up or taken their credit cards off the little plate with the bill on it and pocketed them until the waiter has taken mine only and the bill is paid for.

I have on more than a thousand occasions, taken it too far and **upset** people - which is the absolute *last* thing I ever want to do. Paying for drinks once or twice is not a problem. Doing something nice for someone every now and then is not a bad thing - it is indeed a *good* thing.

Wrestling friends to the ground in order to get the bill off them, is, to be fair sometimes quite funny, but generally it's taking it too far.

Not giving people a *choice* is a **bad** thing.

It is only really in the last four or so years that I have started to notice that I can make people **unhappy** with my need to make them **happy** with stupid over-the-top gestures.

My first awareness of it was when a wonderful couple wanted to take me and ODFOP out for sushi. Knowing me, they had categorically INSISTED before we went in that there was to be no argument when it came to the bill.

I remained mute because that was the very very best I could do - every fibre of my being wanting to tell them that they didn't need to, that I wanted to pay - pleeeeeeassse.

Throughout the whole evening I was plotting and planning how I could pay for it. I hated that time was passing when they thought I was eating things that they were going to be paying for, how rude was it of me to just order another drink, take another plate of the conveyor belt and expect them to pay?? It was literally excruciating for me.

When it came to the bill being counted up (Yo! Sushi where the bowls on the table are counted to calculate the bill) a big jokey fuss was made of them ensuring I didn't get to see it or try and pay it in any way.

These are gorgeous lovely people who just wanted to treat us to a meal.

Inside I was bursting with anguish.

We were all joking about it as we walked to the till to pay. He was distracted chatting and laughing, and I took my only chance. I grabbed the bill from his hand and ran to the till and begged them to take my card and not listen to the others. I was desperately trying to make it into nothing and a bit of a joke, but it turned into a thing.

In the melee, I saw a flash of pain on both their faces.

They weren't enjoying this, they weren't trying to make a "pretend fuss" and let me pay, they were actually hurt. Oh God. I was hurting these people I loved, but I didn't know how to get out of it. **I didn't know how to *not* pay for everyone.**

I pressed on because I was stuck in a pattern I couldn't break, and I apologised and apologised while I paid the bill. They genuinely looked sad - and I had caused it. The evening ended with them accepting my apology, but I was in pieces inside. This was the first time that I recognised that my actions were selfish.

I went and got a therapist.

I came to realise that I have probably embarrassed most of the people I have ever been out with. I learned that I had heard this "if you can do something nice for someone you should do it" mantra and turned it into my palatable excuse for aggressively putting my needs above anyone else's. Like a junkie, after a feel-good fix.

What if someone **else** wanted to be nice? Make a gesture? Be thanked for paying the bill? (I shouldn't I know, but I feel the need to add that it was never about being thanked - for me - it was about thinking I had done something unexpected that made other people happy) What if people didn't **want** to feel like they were being taken out by their mother every time they went out with me? What if people *stopped telling me* what they wanted in life, for fear of me putting it in a box and leaving it on their doorstep - instead of allowing them the enjoyment of working for it, earning it, and choosing it for themselves? What if people stopped arranging to go out for drinks with me because they just *couldn't handle* the agro of trying to share the bill at the end? How many friends had I lost over the years? How many "user" friends had I acquired? People that expected it? I didn't think **anyone** ever expected it, for me **that** was the point...

Used for sex, yes, I knew that one well. That was an *old* way of making people happy, I got the brief fix of "going over and above" what other people would do to make that person happy and also there was a tiny hopeful possibility that during meaningless sex they could decide I was worth loving.

But know if someone *expected* me to pick up the bill, I don't have a clue. I've never given anyone the chance to show that to me.

So, in summary of my deepest, uncomfortable confession, (that is hardly anything to do with ODFOP either - he is still a fucker though) - this is my shame, and my hardest internal battle.

My name is Kate, I am now a recovering people-pleaser. If I get out of control, please use the word ODFOP and I will know I have pushed it too far.

Getting to the step where I make amends to individuals is going to be time consuming...

Would it be wrong to hire Necker Island and take everyone there to apologise all together?

I'm *joking*.... Jeeez...lighten up.

XIII. ODFOP – Grand Master of Cunning

I had always had a desire to take care of some chickens.

This was 10 years ago, just before chickens in the back garden were *de rigueur*.

I like to think of myself as the trendsetter, but it's more likely it was coincidence...

It was a year after my mum had died.

The three of us were living *en famille* at my family home. Cracks were starting to appear in the relationships.

Dad had lived in this house since 1979, when 3 of us kids, mum and he moved in as a family.

He was "set in his ways".

He liked the heating up, the fire on, windows shut, to smoke big cigars and to watch what **he** wanted to watch on telly.

He was used to being picked-up after, and having his food made and delivered to him.

He had always, *always* been a self-centred man.

He **never** suffered from guilt, **never** apologised for anything, and he always did *exactly* what he wanted.

In his prime, he had been a reasonably senior figure in the world of luxury cars. He ruled his fiefdom with the fear of his legendary wrath.

He was absolutely delighted to re-tell the story of when he made a man faint with fear. It was much more likely to be that the chap hadn't eaten or wasn't well, but for dad, it was **fear of him** that made the man pass out.

He was *exceedingly* **proud** of that.

He was an only child and didn't really know how to "interact" in a large family of children. So, he didn't.

He never played with us, he never hugged us or told us he loved us. Affection was not his thing. Discipline, that was his thing. He was **keen** on that.

Once, in 1979, waaaaay back when there were 3 channels and you couldn't pause telly, AND no video recorders for normal people. You watched it or missed it. *Dark dark* days.

I was early teens, and I had a complete crush on **Gary Numan**. OMG I loved him.

He was **never** on the telly, except for occasionally, Top of the Pops.

One Sunday afternoon, we were all watching telly and the in-between-programme-announcer said that there was about to be a short programme on Gary Numan, something about his flying.

I was *beside* myself with excitement.

Dad ordered me to make him a cup of tea - now. I got up and stood by the lounge door, watching the telly as it started.

"Don't make me tell you again!" he shouted.

I went and put a pan of water on the stove (we had no kettle) and came back, watching it by the lounge door.

"you had better not have left that water on the stove". I edged a bit further back, so I could watch the pan **and** the telly.

The next thing I knew my father was in front of me.

He grabbed my plaits and yanked me backwards so hard that I fell over. "get up right now and make my tea" he said in a voice that threatened **so** much worse.

"but, it's **Gary Numan!**" I wailed.

Shit.

I remember my brother looking at me in shock - I had answered dad back.

now I was for it.

I was pulled up to standing by my plaits. He simultaneously smacked me on both sides of my head with his flat palms. My head was spinning. The ringing and pain in my ears was terrible.

He pulled me by the plaits to the stove and watched me, sobbing, make him a cup of tea. He then walked back into the lounge and shut the door on me.

I was not allowed back in. I was crying so loudly my mum came out. She came and looked at me. She called my father.

There was blood in one of my ears. His handprints were visible on my cheeks. "What have you done?" my mother said to him "look at her face. Her ear is bleeding!".

"Do you think she needs taking to the hospital?" said my dad as though it was *perfectly normal* to need to take your child to A&E for not making a cup of tea quickly enough. They decided I didn't need to go and I was sent to my room for the rest of the day.

I remember recounting this story to ODFOP once.

Thinking back on it, I was just so gutted that I missed Gary Numan; I wasn't angry or upset that I had been so badly bullied by my father. It was the 70's. We thought that was **normal**.

ODFOP had many equally horrible stories of his father to tell.

Anyhow, my father, self-centred and living now (officially/technically) in mine and my husband's house.

What could *possibly* go wrong?

The amicable relationship lasted just over a year. ODFOP's anger at my father's oblivious-to-anyone-else-existing ways was growing steadily.

I spent a **lot** of energy trying to cover up or take the blame for, anything that might be seen by ODFOP as my father being selfish.

Left a towel on the floor? "oh sorry, that was me"

Left stilton crumbs on the kitchen table? - "oh sorry, I made dad a sandwich and just forgot to wipe up"

Dad smoking a cigar without shutting the lounge door "oh sorry, he did ask me to close it, I just didn't check it was shut"

Dad's Fixodent all over the bathroom sink "oh gosh, that's me again. I told him not to worry and that I would clean it, and then I forgot"

If ever anyone ever deserved to have worn and old-style Kings Fool outfit, it was me. I hopped from foot to foot, deflecting, absorbing, catching and sticking down my top a million things to try and keep the peace.

I took the blame for these two men doing things they frankly **wanted** to be seen to be doing as a "fuck you" to each other.

It was exhausting.

One Sunday we were all sitting on the patio having lunch. We had dug the back half of the garden into a nice allotment and it was growing lots of vegetables for us.

I said out loud "I'd really like to get some chickens".

"Over my dead body" said my father.

It turns out that ODFOP was just about to say the same thing, but then my father said it first.

A cunning plan to piss my father off hatched like a tiny chick in ODFOP's mind.

"Well, I think we should look into it" he said.

Unaware of this tiny peep-peep-peeping chick in ODFOP's mind, I was amazed and delighted at his response.

"You're not getting bloody chickens" repeated my father

"um, I don't think it's up to you" said ODFOP.

"it bloody well is" said my father, now getting a bit annoyed

ODFOP turned to me and said, "we will look into it".

I had no idea of what was really going on, but I clapped my hands with delight and got my laptop immediately.

The whole "who is Alpha Male Gorilla thing had properly kicked off - except neither of them were Alpha Males, they were both Beta males, at best. So, the beta to alpha competition was on.

Six weeks later, we got 2 chickens, Henny and Cuckoo. They were the beginning of an ever-growing passion for me.

This was the first time **anyone** apart from my mother had openly gone against my father that I knew of.

I was slightly in awe of ODFOP. I genuinely thought he had protected me from my father and was letting me get chickens because he knew I wanted them.

Hahaha! I know. Naïve doesn't even *start* to cover it.

Hindsight is a bastard. You can see it all as clear as day and there is NOTHING you can do about it.

Finding new ways of showing my father he could basically "go fuck himself" (without ever being so *obvious* as to *tell* him of course), became a bit of a *raison detre* for ODFOP.

His "wins" started off small and were very crafty and petty.

Maybe getting him the wrong sweeteners when we went food shopping, or the wrong apples or pears. He

147

was very good, because I didn't have a clue what he was up to.

He would look down the shopping list and find things my father wanted, and he would helpfully, go off "in search" of them.

If I'd ask where it was, it was "out of stock",

if I was distracted, he wouldn't say anything, because mentally I had ticked it off as in the trolley.

Every trip, there was something of dad's that we hadn't bought or was wrong. I just put it down to me being forgetful.

Tiny, pathetic wins. But wins all the same.

There was a phase where ODFOP would pretend not to hear him.

He started wearing ear phones in his ears a lot at home. If I spoke, he heard me, if my father spoke, he would pretend that he didn't hear a thing.

If I questioned him about the inconsistency, I was wrong. "How on earth do you know whether what I can hear or not?"

My father would get up early and exercise every morning. ODFOP started to time it so it was about 30 seconds before my father was done and ready to get into the shower, and he would duck into the bathroom and lock the door and sit there for *ages*.

If my father banged on the door he would tell him to "fuck off" and that he was "having a shit", and he would take *even longer*. He would then come to me and moan to me that my father was a rude fucker. I would say to him, "if you need to go to the loo at that time, just go downstairs". His answer was always, "why should I?"

"Why should I?" was said *a lot* by ODFOP when I asked him to be considerate of my father.

Sodding hindsight. If there was to be a theme running through our time together in this house with my father, it was that if there was a situation that needed compromise and I asked him to do the compromising, it was "why should I? Why doesn't your arrogant fucking father do ......?".

It was crafted and delivered in such a way that I genuinely felt that I was **constantly** asking *him* to give way, and he would *always* give way, until this **one time** when he said, "why should I?". **I** was the one being unreasonable, by continually badgering him, and not my father.

Except I **always** asked both of them, and ODFOP **never** gave way. It just sounded like he always did.

That said, my father was the same. I would ask him to compromise on something and he would give me a very good reason why ODFOP should compromise instead. He would say to me "you *know* he is in the wrong" and I would say "I don't know he is in the wrong at all".

Eventually they stopped talking all together. ODFOP had ignored my father one too many times with his ear phones in, declaring that he didn't hear him, and they had a row. My father was raging, banging his hand on the table, demanding that ODFOP apologised. ODFOP was calm and said he had nothing to apologise for.

That's when it got unbearable. Maybe 14 months into our living together.

So, no meals together any more. ODFOP bought a telly and sat in our bedroom. I sat half with my father and half with ODFOP, feeling very in the middle.

It soon became the norm for my father to eat in the lounge, me to eat in the kitchen and ODFOP to eat in our bedroom.

I had begged both of them to work it out.

"he should apologise to me" they would both say.

My father was keener on making amends than ODFOP, but he was still quite proud - having never really had to apologise for anything before then. But when he agreed to apologise for the sake of the atmosphere, I ran to ODFOP. "he will apologise!" I was so delighted and relieved! This nightmare was going to be over, finally!

"I don't want to talk to that wanker" ODFOP said.

A fifty-tonne lead weight fell on me.

"What??? he said he'd apologise!!".

"It's too late. It shouldn't take you to tell him to apologise, he should've done it weeks ago".

That was that.

And it was my fault that I had been darting between them trying to make it work - apparently, I was "making a meal out of it".

So, maybe a peaceful truce where they don't talk could now fall into place? Just keep out of each other's way?

Hahaha! again. Hindsight you can **fuck right off.**

Things of my fathers started going missing. Food, shirts, a gold ring, towels from the bathroom.

Dad would tell me ODFOP had done it.

ODFOP would tell me he was losing his mind, "why would I do that?". And it was such a petty stupid thing, that I would think, "he's right! why on earth would he do something so banal and petty? Dad's mistaken"

ODFOP was *good* at it, there was **never** any evidence. Never *anything* concrete, to say he had done anything wrong. He was very *very* good at getting annoyed at being "falsely accused".

Lucky for him, I was very *very* good at **not** pressing the point or having any confidence in my belief.

151

I never really believed that he did any of those things, because if he did do those things, then how awful a person was he? I couldn't have fallen in love with a man like that?

Therefore, my father was innocently mistaken, and whatever it was will turn up - and there will be a perfectly logical explanation for it.

Lalala the **Powerful**.

Sometimes "it" turned up exactly where it had been missing from for days. Sometimes it would be somewhere ridiculous, sometimes it was never seen again.

My father had a belt buckle gold ring. He didn't tell me it was missing, but I happened to find it one day in a tiny pot on a high shelf in the kitchen.

I took it in to my father "what was this doing on the top shelf in a pot?".

"I didn't put it there"

"You must have. No-one else would have had it"

"I. did. not. put. it. there."

"ok, but there is no other explanation for it being there"

"ODFOP put it there"

"why would he do that?"

"Because he is hiding things from me"

152

"I don't think he is dad, but anyway, it's back now, so it's all good"

Me to ODFOP "Did you hide dad's gold ring in the top of the cupboard in a tiny pot?"

"no. what gold ring?"

"his belt buckle one"

"I didn't know he had a belt buckle one. He's losing his mind"

"how would it have got there though?"

"how would I know?"

"ok"

I had that conversation with ODFOP maybe 100 times a year for the nine remaining years my father lived with us.

I did catch him once.

My father liked scones. He'd eat packets of them.

Once, when I left the kitchen for a few minutes (taking dad a cup of tea into the lounge and then chatting to him). I came back and went into the pantry as he'd asked for a scone.

I noticed that two of the scones in the packet in the pantry were blue and mouldy.

The date on the packet said they were still fresh.

My father would **never** have looked at the scone - he would have picked it up and shoved it in his mouth without inspecting it.

Shocked, I said "Oh My God, these scones are mouldy! how can they be mouldy when it says they are still in date? That's terrible. I'm, going to take those back to Tesco first thing tomorrow. I can't believe that - dad could've eaten those"

ODFOP stayed silent.

For once, out of a million fails, HOAM got through to me, over the Lalala's one-man brass band.

ODFOP had been in the kitchen the whole time cleaning up after Sunday dinner.

Where had the fresh scones that had been removed out of the packet, gone to?

I could see ODFOP watching me as he dried up a pan. I opened up the food recycling bin on the counter. Just sprout and parsnip peelings....

HOAM got another word through. I lifted up the peelings - and there were 2 squashed fresh scones...

"What on earth?" I said to ODFOP.

His best defence has always been confident deflection.

"What?" very crossly, "I didn't put them there, it's probably your father".

Five hundred times before, that had been enough for me.

Why would my husband lie to me over something so stupid?

Lalala says, non comprendre - the other option was just *too awful*.

But this time I stuck to my guns, *very* nervously...

"You *did* put them there - what on *earth* were you *thinking?* that's a terrible thing to do. *Why* would you do that?"

"I told you, *I didn't fucking put them there*" - with venom and malice this time.

You may recall from my other posts, I don't like an unhappy atmosphere... I was clearly being threatened with "If you pursue this, I will make your life very uncomfortable, for a *very long time"*

I **knew** I was being threatened with that too.

The whole magnitude of actually catching him out - and the consequences of that - was too much to cope with. Lalala added *MUCH more wine* to her arsenal.

It was easier than facing the truth.

XIV. ODFOP AND OTHER ANIMALS PART 1

ODFOP has never really understood my *need* to care for animals.

He vaguely recalls having a cat for a while when he was a child, but it just left one day, and that was that. They didn't have a cat anymore. No gut wrenching tears and anguish, or even mild worry. No knocking on neighbour's doors, taping up posters on lampposts, calling all the local vets, no searching the streets at night with a torch calling the cats name. "It just didn't come back".

"Making a fuss" was very much disapproved of in ODFOP's family home - but even knowing that, he told me doesn't remember having any affection for it. It was just their cat. Until it wasn't.

We *always* had a pet as part of the family. Mostly dogs, but periods with a cat, tortoises, hedgehogs, and gerbils. They were a key part of our family life and we all loved them - except dad. He loved the dogs I think, but he *commanded* them - and they obeyed. Much like his kids.

I had my own cat when I was young and very innocent.

I named her "Pussy".

Oh yes, I did.

I can't imagine my life *without* animals around me. It's an honour and a privilege to look after an animal that is dependent on humans for food and comfort. I think every child should have that experience. A pet's love is unconditional.

Unless of course they're a cat. Most cats will bestow upon you mild indifference. A bit of love and you're forever chasing that Nirvana. I expect a cat's affection has much in common with heroin. I am blessed to have had the honour of being owned by some very special cats in my time.

I would love to be as confident in myself as a cat is. It's not even confidence. It's *beyond* confidence. It's utter unshakeable knowledge that it is a **fact**. To just **know** that I was superior - to **everything** and everyone around me. I can't even *see* what that **looks** like, let alone sense or taste it. That kind of confidence is like trying to imagine what is at the end of space.

I wonder if that's how Donald Trump feels? Is Donald Trump a cat?

It's a shame that we can't go to a shop and try on new personality traits. Step into a fleecy onesie and

instantly you're comfortable in your own skin. Try on a clown suit and your brain is thinking of new jokes and you are simply *hilarious*. Maybe an anxious person could buy a Rastafarian outfit and immediately be chilled and laid back. An athletes outfit, and you're instantly thinking about being fit and healthy. Maybe there would a Donald Trump suit. Actually, no - that's taking things too far. I think Madonna should possibly be the most confident outfit you should be able to get - and maybe that should only be available for short term hire - to discourage misuse. If we were all inhabiting Madonna's confidence, who would be our entourage?

No, thinking it through, maybe there should be something like Total Recall, or Eternal Sunshine of the Spotless Mind. Have things inserted or removed from your brain.

I can see a Shopping Channel, like JML -Christmas adverts could be **so** much more *interesting*.

Cue, talking-slightly-too-fast man's voice speaking *very* enthusiastically...

"Eaten too many mince pies and *still* can't stop reaching for that tin of Quality Street? Can't fit into those favourite Skinny Jeans?

Skinny Thinking!™ was created just for you!

Buy and install our **Skinny Thinking!**™ implant. It's a simple painless process! No down time! Instant Results!

We'll even remove that unhelpful **Comfort Eating Makes Me Happy** programme and dispose of it, *free of charge*!

That's right folks! With our patented **Skinny Thinking!**™ implant, instantly you will know when you are full, only ever eat what is good for you, and have no problem saying "no" to that second helping!

It's Amazing!

But Wait! There's more!

Why not take advantage of our three for two offer? Buy **Skinny Thinking!**™ and **I *Really* Want to Exercise**™, and get **Witty Repartee**™ or **Fluent Italian**™ *for free*!

That's a £22,000 value, for ***Only £12,000.***

Easy payment plans available. skinnythinkingimplantmustbeimplantedinoneofourac creditedstoresappointmentsavailablefor£2000seriousl ookingpeopleinwhitecoatswillperformtheimplantandr emovalbutwedonotguaranteethattheyhavehadanytrai ningwhatsoever.newbrainencorporated™doesnotacce ptanyliabilityforunsuccessfulimplantsorforanybotched removalsofcomforteatingprogramme.82percentofourc ustomershavehadhardlyanylastingbraindamage.

Ok, enough silliness. That'll be the pickled onions talking. Pickled onion, lettuce, cucumber, vegan mayonnaise and Tofurky sandwich on Boxing Day. Oooh yessssss.

Anyway, animals. I have had the honour of looking after a few special animals in my life.

Moses (aka Moses Supposes, Mosapose, MoMo) was a black cat from Cats Protection League. My friend Sam spotted him. Crammed in a pen with 20 other cats, his purr was loud, and his face was beautiful. As soon as she pointed him out and I set eyes on him, he looked at me like he had been expecting me, and he was so pleased I was here to take him home. A bit like that Dogs Trust advert on the telly where the dogs have a stuffed toy that looks like their owner. He would sit on my chest and bat my eyes with his un-clawed paw if I stopped looking at him or I shut them.

Susie (aka Squeezy, Squeezawooze, Squeedle). My sister spotted her at the animal sanctuary. She was miserable. A beautiful girl. She lived until she was 21 and never aged from when she was about 5. (this is here at 21 - I know! maybe the Fountain of Youth is in my back garden?)

She didn't like many people. Certainly, hated ODFOP. Clever cat. Never thought to let me in on it.

Too many chickens to name, Henny and Cuckoo started me off and it was a slow but steady snowballing effect from there.

I know a girl should never admit she had a favourite chicken, but I did. Her name was **Joanna** and she was a rescue ex-battery hen. She had confidence and joie *de* *vivre* that just made you smile. If she didn't have a beak, she would've just been grinning, day and night.

Most ex-battery hens are terrible bullies of other chickens. They've had to fight in a tiny cage for 18 months for every bit of space and every bit of food. They've never learned to relax, or share. They come to you featherless, exhausted, weak and beaten down. To watch them learn to walk around, flap their wings and peck at a piece of sweetcorn for the first time is enough to make a mortal man burst with both joy and sorrow.

Joanna was just such a fun bird. She would sit on my lap in the sunshine, and purr. Oh yes, happy chickens purr.

Then there was **Fox in Sox**

Fox in Sox was my pal. I used to have a wire fence around the grass in the garden, so the chickens could wander round free during the day.

One day I came out into the garden and I notice the fence was "jerking". Behind a tree, a fox cub had got its head caught in the fencing and had wound it round its neck so tightly it was strangling itself. I grabbed some scissors and while the terrified cub tried to get away from me, I started to cut her free. She had a huge welt round her neck and had rubbed her fur off. As soon as she was free she scarpered. I never thought I would see her again.

But then she started visiting. And she got braver and braver.

At our peak she would sit beside me in the garden with the chickens wandering around her, just happy and content. I hand fed her most days, for over eight years. We went through several pregnancies, mange, tics, territory fights, and boyfriends (all hers, not mine). She would come into the house in the summer if we'd left the French windows open, just to let me know she was there. When we had some work going on in the house and the front door and French windows were open, she would just trot right through.

She liked hotdogs from Costco best. She was also partial to jam on toast (good for getting mange tablets down her). When we'd go on holiday, the house-sitter was instructed on how to feed her. She would send me photos. She (Fox in Sox, not the House-sitter) had a lovely boyfriend for the last few years, a real gentleman. He would always let her eat first, especially when she was pregnant. He'd stay back until I went back into the house and then trot down. He'd sit beside her until she's finished eating, and then eat the last of the food. They'd then trot off back up the garden together.

Sometime in June 2017 was the last time I saw her. It went from seeing them both, and perhaps one or two of their off spring every day, to nothing. For weeks. I was distraught. I spoke to the Fox Project to see if they had any new rescues from my area, I called the council to see if anyone had been complaining about foxes. I even rang some "pest" control companies to see if they had been working in the area. Nothing. It must've been a month with no foxes at all. That hadn't happened for the last 10 years.

Then one day I'd been working late. It was about 7.30 and I was on the train, miserable, thinking about Fox in Sox.

My phone went ping! ODFOP had sent me a WhatsApp.

I opened it up and the message said, "is this your fox?"

It was Fox in Sox's boyfriend! The first fox back in our garden for over a month!

A loud sob escaped, and tears ran down my face. "are you ok?" the woman next to me said, thinking I may have just got some really bad news or something. "Yes!

Yes! Fox in Sox's boyfriend is back!" I sobbed/blurted. I shoved my phone under her nose "look! he's back!" She smiled a slightly awkward smile and carried on reading her kindle.

I spent the rest of the journey stroking my phone, grinning like a loon, wiping my eyes and fighting the urge to tell the rest of the train. I really was **that** happy. I thought someone had trapped and killed them all.

I like to think that Fox in Sox had just got very old and he had nursed her at home until the end. He'd then gone off travelling in order to grieve and get his head straight. When he was ready, he came home.

I feed Fox in Sox's boyfriend most days. He will come and sit in the garden, so the light sensors go off and I can see he's there, or he'll just sit patiently if I'm not there or if I haven't seen him. Sometimes I am sitting watching the telly and I just get the feeling I am being watched, and I'll look in the garden and he's there. Staring at me. He prefers Pedigree Chum. He has a new girlfriend who he sometimes brings for dinner. He always lets her eat first. She's not a classy as Fox in Sox, but there will never be another.

XV. ODFOP AND OTHER ANIMALS PART 2

After Squeezy died, it was a full, endless 24-hour period before I couldn't stand the silence in the house any longer.

I spoke to my BM who understands about cats "is it too soon?"

"Oh, good god no, I lasted no more than 2 days and they were both hell".

Off me and ODFOP went to Foal Farm in search of a new love for me. I was allowed 2 cats, because I had Squeezy and Mosapose at the same time for several years.

I got three.

George and Otto came first and George's mum Izzy, followed shortly after when she had weaned her kittens.

George and his mum had been inseparable before she got up the duff again... I think **he** was possibly their brother **and** their father, but the less said about that the better.

Otto had joined the ticket because George had made friends with him in his little cat run.

Otto was magnificent. A pure breed Turkish Angora and was only a year old. Big, fluffy white and with piercing blue eyes. Apparently, his owner was unable to take care of him as she was ill. I can't imagine having to give up any of my animals, ever. It must've been heart breaking - he was barely out of kitten-hood. George and his mum were part of a big group of cats that weren't being looked after properly and the couple had split up, neither of them wanting to take on the cats. George's mum was pregnant, and George was only 8 months old, Izzy was just fourteen months and already on her second litter.

Otto and ODFOP bonded immediately.

In the time it took me to go out and get some special cat food and toys for them, the brief window of opportunity for Otto's affections had opened and closed. I was shut out. Otto would lay luxuriously up ODFOP's body like a sash. Any attempt to entice him over to me was met with a blank stare of indifference.

I was stumped. This had *never* happened before. ODFOP was not so discreetly, smug about it. He had never been given affection by any animal.

I couldn't help it, I begrudged him.

Mosesapose and Squeedle disliked ODFOP intensely and they **loved** me. Bruce our bantam cockerel (who actually thinking about him makes me realise I loved him above *all* other chickens - Bruce tales to follow) all disliked ODFOP.

I was the bloody animal person in the house. What was *going on*?

I tried desperately to get his affection, but he was giving none of it.

He had never been outside before he came to us and spend days and weeks encouraging him to come in to the garden and taste some real freedom. I brushed him regularly, so he didn't get knotty. I bought him the best food, cat towers to climb on, and I told him how beautiful he was and how much I loved him. But, for whatever reason, I just leave Otto the psychopathic cat, cold.

To this day if I am sitting in the lounge and with, as far as he is concerned a total stranger, he will jump up on their lap and purr. He has only **once** put his paw on me with anything like affection, and that was for less than a minute. He is like Kevin, in We Need to Talk About Kevin. I am Tilda Swinton in this scenario.

He is currently in love with our lodger - who has even said *in front of him* that she is a DOG PERSON. Bastard cat. I saved him from the rescue place - muttermutter in a Mutley kind of way...

Anyway, I am now reminiscing about **Bruce**, bollocks to Otto.

Let me share with you the story of this little King.

He was a Bantam, which is just a miniature chicken - about half the size of a normal chicken when fully grown. Friends of ours had some gorgeous little bantam hens and got me some too. I didn't know at the time, but in order to get the girls, they had to buy a boy with them as a breeding trio. They were happy to keep the boy as he was a pure breed and they could breed from him. But he missed his girls. He apparently was moping round in his pen, looking forlorn.

So we had a trial of keeping a cockerel. He was only maybe 7 weeks old when he joined us. About a quarter of the size of the full-grown hens.

In nature, a cockerel will keep the hens in check, and as far as pecking order goes, he will be the boss-man. Bruce, being tiny, couldn't really round up his harem of full sized girls. But it didn't stop him trying, the little pocket rocket. He would chase them all mercilessly, trying desperately to get them to do his bidding. They were having none of it. A few of them would just stand their ground and give him a sharp peck on his head in a swatting-an-annoying-fly kind of way.

He, however, was an eternal optimist, and I loved him for that. He was a gentle, gorgeous boy who would fall

168

asleep in the palm of my hand as I gently stroked his comb.

Then testosterone happened.

One of his girls needed some medicine and ODFOP and I were administering it to her. She was mildly unhappy and was flapping a bit.

Bruce was beside himself. He was darting around, looking at what he could do to protect his girl.

ODFOP said "he's going to peck me"

I said "no, he's a sweetie, he wouldn't hurt a fly".

Suddenly, ODFOP's hand had a small chunk out of it and was bleeding profusely.

Shocked I looked at ODFOP. Both his and my mouth were perfect O's. Then I started laughing. The kind of laugh that makes your stomach muscles ache and your eyes stream.

ODFOP's voice was getting higher "He's going to peck me again, stop him!" but I was unable to do anything.

The red mist had descended, and Bruce was suddenly a GIANT. Full of rage. He had real **bloodlust**.

He jumped onto ODFOP and was pecking his arm like his life depended on it.

"GET HIM OFF ME!!" ODFOP was now shrieking. but I couldn't - the sight of this tiny half pint cockerel going berserk on ODFOP, who was desperately trying to brush him off, and Bruce was pecking his hand whenever it got close to him, was just hilarious!

Thirty seconds later, I composed myself long enough to pick him off ODFOP. He was struggling in my hands, and his little legs were going in a kind of "just let me at him, pud 'em uuup, I'll rip his heart out with my beak, just give me two minutes alone with him" way.

ODFOP was bleeding all over the place, and was I think in shock.

I turned away to stifle my sniggers and stroked Bruce's comb until he calmed down and fell asleep in my hands.

After that ODFOP couldn't go near him. If all the chickens were out and I was gardening at the back on the allotment part, and Bruce saw ODFOP walking up from the house, the mist would descend again, and he would charge at him all the way down the garden ending in a high karate kick. He pecked chunks out of his wellies, his legs (through jeans) and once took a chunk out of his chin.

It got to the point that whenever ODFOP went into the chicken's house, he had to put a bucket over Bruce. This furious up-turned bucket would be jumping, as Bruce tried desperately to get free and murder ODFOP.

He was indomitable. A tiny boy, no more than 12 inches tall from claws to comb, with the heart and courage of a bull elephant. The only trouble was Bruce wanted to tell the world where he was and that he would fight anyone who was up for it. From about 3.00 a.m. to about 10.30 p.m. Pretty much non-stop. His crowing was legendary.

Sadly, a group of sleep-deprived neighbours complained to the council and he had to be rehomed.

Bruce was a legend in his own lifetime. I still miss him.

ODFOP and I got into the habit of going to Corfu twice a year for the last 5 years of our marriage. We loved North East Corfu in particular. We would rent a villa and just chill. For the most part, when you rent a villa, you rent a couple of cats too. They come as a package deal. It got to the point where we would stop off at the Lidl near the airport after we'd pick up the hire car, and stock up on cat biscuits and little trays of wet food in anticipation.

I also learned to take a few trays of wet food and a bag of biscuits in my handbag for when we went out. There were always lots of strays just hoping for a bite to eat from a passing tourist.

Quite often I would take myself off while ODFOP sunbathed at the villa stopping by the bins to feed the strays. Our favourite restaurant we even referred to as "the cat restaurant" because there were so many cats wandering the tables looking for the odd prawn tail. Taverna Kerasia is a beautiful open-air restaurant. ODFOP would always get the seafood platter and I would always badger him for the whiting heads and tails for the puskies.

I liked to think of it as a tradition. ODFOP said I was just annoying.

On the way there and on the way back I would stop for strays, put the hazard lights on and jump out with my bag of cat food.

Anyway, it was habit. On Holiday, always carry cat food in your bag.

July 2017. I went with my sister and her grown up kids to Marrakesh for a week's holiday in villa. July in Marrakesh is only mildly less mad than July in Luxor, Egypt. It was hot and dusty.

Our villa, Villa Yasmina, was a little compound of paradise. Tortoises, rabbits, dogs, frogs, and cats roamed the beautiful gardens.

On the first Monday afternoon most of us decided to go to the souk at Jeema El Fna, the main square. I took a big raffia shopping bag and of course, some cat biscuits and water.

We were on our way, looking out of the window, as you do. I spotted a tiny kitten scramble up the ditch toward a man and his small son, who were walking down the side of the road. The man kicked it back into the ditch.

Sharp intake of breath. "What's wrong?" said my sister "that man just kicked a kitten into the ditch". We carried on in silence for 30 seconds, digesting what I had seen, and thinking about what we could actually do about it in a strange country where animals are rarely pets.

"Can you turn around please" burst out of my mouth. Suddenly it was urgent.

"What? are you *sure*?" the taxi driver said

"absolutely" I said.

We turned around at the next round about and drove back to where we had seen the kitten. The taxi driver found him and picked him up. We was absolutely tiny, covered in dust and had one eye closed. No mum or siblings to be seen, so I took him back into the taxi.

He couldn't have been more than four weeks old and he looked exhausted. As we continued on our journey, he wolfed down the biscuits I offered to him and drank his weight in water. I dampened down a tissue and tried to clean his eyes.

His purr resonated throughout the inside of the car.

When we got to the Souk, I bought a cheap scarf and put it in the bottom of my big shopping bag. The kitten curled up and slept all the way round the souk. Still purring.

We got back to the villa and gave him some wet food and I soaked the cat biscuits, so they were easier to digest.

His belly full and now out of danger, this little kitten came to life.

He was just the happiest, most inquisitive, playful bundle of cuteness anyone could ever have had the absolute pleasure of spending some time with.

How could a tiny kitten, who was probably only hours from dying in a hot dusty ditch by the side of a road, blossom into a tiny furry treasure in a matter of moments?

We thought of many names for him - initially thinking he was a her, we thought Yasmina after the villa, then another name, then another.

I decided on Jaqen H'ghar after the rather handsome man in Game of Thrones. "A man has no name".

Finally however, we decided on Yoda. For one very good reason. He was mostly made of ears.

I found a vet to get him checked over, and got a timetable planned and paid for upfront for him to have all his injections and testing so he could come over to the UK.

He spent the whole week with us in the villa, sleeping with me at night and playing and sleeping during the day.

We all fell hopelessly in love with him.

The family that looked after the villa, kindly agreed to keep him safe and take him to the vets' appointments and I gave them money for his food, taxi's to the vets and their time.

On the last day of our holiday my sister and I sobbed our heads off. It was 7th July and we couldn't bring him over to the UK until 1st December. It was FOREVER to wait. I had no more available holiday time with work to even come for a weekend. I was going to have to ask for an unpaid day in December to come and get him as it was.

We booked our flights back the day we got home, and I started looking into how to get him over to the UK.

Oh. My. Good. God. So much misinformation, misdirection, unspoken rules and regulations to wade through. Not even people who import pets for a living could help us. Morocco was just a huge No. No. I spent nearly £1,000 on getting advice or wrong information. One company said, just bring him over, he can spend his time in quarantine in the UK, it's easy! £300 to get a license to bring a non-compliant animal into the UK. Got that. Book his passage on a flight. Another £300. Airline needs license number. Ring back with the licence number and am told my someone else that that airline did not have clearance to fly animals from Morocco to the UK.

"No, the ticket you purchased was non-refundable"

"Well, we can't put absolutely everything on our website".

"The person you spoke to before was incorrect - if you bring your animal to fly on our airline, he will not be allowed on board"

"crying is unfortunately not going to change the airlines policy on this madam"

"I don't know what that means, but I think I am going to terminate this call now, goodbye".

I spoke to Royal Air Maroc, British Airways, Lufthansa, Air France, EasyJet, Ryan Air, Thomson, and Norwegian Air International. I rang their Moroccan desks, I spoke to their air freight subsidiaries. I spoke in appalling French, and even worse Arabic and cried on the phone to at least 6 different people. My sister was amazing and went down several other rabbit holes of information to try and get him over. The is no one trail of information to follow that gets your cat from Marrakesh to Kent. There is a spider's web of information, spun by a drunk spider, and then a flock of albatrosses have flown through it.

I shit you not, my hair started falling out. It was hideous.

It got to a point where I was properly seriously thinking about calling in sick, flying to Marrakesh, sewing him into the lining of my coat, getting a ferry to Gibraltar and hitchhiking across Europe and then smuggling him across from Calais to Dover.

I looked at ferries crossings.

All through this time, the wonderful family were sending me photos of Yoda, looking happy and playful.

Then they sent me one of him curled up on a little girls' arm, looking very content.

I was jealous.

But I had to ask the question. I WhatsApp back "do you love him?"

I prayed that they would say "no". She WhatsApp called me straight away. Her young sisters were squealing in the background and she shushed them.

"yes, we love him" she said.

Oh fuckedybollocks.

"Then you should keep him, if you **really** want to".

She had obviously made some gesture to the girls like thumbs up or a nod as they started screaming and laughing in the background.

"bastards" I thought.

We went to see him on 1 December, because we had the flights booked anyway.

We agreed that if we spotted *anything* at all wasn't right or he recognised us and wanted to come with us, we would bring him home in our hand luggage.

He was, however, a happy 7-month-old prince who has a large house in Marrakesh and several servants that fulfil his every wish. Of course, he didn't recognise us, and he loved the children.

I was **gutted**.

After rescuing Yoda, me and ODFOP went for what was to be our last holiday in Corfu together. Usual cat foot contingency acquired near the airport, we stopped at the Villa Plus office on our way past to drop of some bits to the staff, who by now had become good and fabulous friends. They told us of a cat at the villa just being knocked over and killed that morning and her kitten being alone now. The villa owner was looking for the kitten and was going to take it. I took a sharp intake of breath and raised my hand up to speak. ODFOP shot me a glance (he hadn't forgiven me for deciding to bring Yoda from Marrakesh without "consulting" him which in reality means, giving him a chance to say "NO") and I stifled my urges.

We continued our drive to the villa. I couldn't speak because I was bursting with wanting to take care of this kitten. Half way there and I couldn't hold it in. "Ring them. Ring them now and tell them I will take care of the kitten".

I drive when we are in Corfu as ODFOP lost his confidence after we skidded on a mountain road and smashed (luckily) into the wall, rather than going over the cliff...

He muttered several expletives under his breath as he dialled our friends. "she says she wants to take care of the kitten. I don't know if she means just for the week or forever. She'll probably have a house built for it and hire staff". ODFOP was genuinely seething. I was desperate to get to the poor kitten who needed love and comfort.

We got to the house and the owner was there, looking for the kitten.

When it comes to kittens or cats, I have bat-like hearing. I could hear very feint mewling in the garden.

I left ODFOP to unpack the car, grabbed the cat food and ran to the garden. There he was. It was like Yoda all over again. Again, maybe only four weeks old - too young to be away from his mum. I scooped him up and hardly put him down for the following week. OMG I *cherished* him. I spent the entire week on my iPad trying to find out how to get a kitten from Corfu to Kent - it **had** to be easier, right? So many stray animals in one country - surely, they would make it easy to ship them to another country?

He had to be 12 weeks old before he could come, and by the time he was 12 weeks old there were no more direct flights from London to Corfu. He would have to

179

go Freight on two flights. Too much to put a three-month-old kitten through.

The owner of the house agreed to take him.

By this time my heart had been stretched to a point where it had a kitten shaped space in it that kept getting filled, and then smashed.

I *needed* a kitten. I told ODFOP. Little did I know he was past caring, so I was told I could do what I liked.

Excellent! I'll get two then.

So, I looked for kittens on gumtree.com. Oh, my good lord. Never mind the complications or risks of investing in Wheat/Gold/Diamond Futures, Kittens are a booming cash cow. Most non-pedigree standard cute-as-a-button kittens were £220 each!! I really hoped that people weren't getting their cats pregnant just to make money - but some probably are.

I also registered with the RSPCA, Cats Protection, Foal Farm, and Battersea Dogs and Cats Home.

Then I spotted them. Two kittens. Sisters. Eight weeks old. They were **gorgeous.** A snip at £80 each. I texted immediately.

We would get home on Saturday morning, I could collect them on Saturday afternoon?

Yes, that would work. Yippee! I had my next kitten fix, they were adorable, and they were in the right country! I couldn't wait to get home.

We drove to a tiny flat in Southwark and knocked on the door.

A giant and very muscly black man in a singlet and shorts opened the door. He looked cross. I looked upwards at his face and said weakly "um. I'm here for the kittens?" It just was so obvious that I had knocked on the wrong door. This man, **was not** a kitten kind of man. This was how I was going to die. I had often wondered how it would happen. I never would have guessed that it would be knocking on the door of an 8ft man while trying to adopt kittens.

His face broke into a huge grin and he said, "come in come in! they're waiting for you!". Neither of us dared exchange glances, so we entered the tiny flat. Stacked in the hallway was body building protein shakes and weights.

In a tiny living room, stacked with cardboard boxes, were these two tiny girls. He picked them up. They looked like mice in his huge hands. He was tickling them under their chins and they were clearly very happy with him. "Aren't they *adorable*?" he said as he handed them to me. The scene was as incongruent as you could get.

"I'm keeping their brother. Their mum got herself knocked up just as I was about to get her neutered - I couldn't not let her have them. They've been brilliant to have around. Will you send me pictures of them growing up?"

"yes of course" I said, looking round for *any* signs that children or a partner lived with him, just *something* that made this man having kittens make sense. Nothing. It was all protein shakes and weights.

"oh, come here" he said as he took them from me and kissed them both on the end of their noses "I'm going to miss you guys!" he said in a tiny high-pitched version of his voice. I looked at ODFOP. He was as stunned as I was. I gave him the cash and he put them in our basket. I said they would be loved and treasured and in his normal voice "they'd better be".

"oh fuck, did I give him our home address?" flashed through my mind.

As we walked out through the front door, I turned and thanked him again. He was bent down, waving at the kittens in the carry cage, grinning from ear to ear. "Don't forgot to send me pictures" he said. He then closed the door.

We were half way home before either of us could speak. "well, *that* was unexpected" said ODFOP.

I send pictures. Regularly.

XVI. Shopping Sans ODFOP

My hairdryer packed up yesterday. A hairdryer is just one those things I can't do without in life.

Not that I have long glossy locks or anything. Far from it. My hair is the perfect combination of greasy at the roots, dry at the ends, and dull in the middle.

Growing up I used to be able to sit on my hair. A hair cut for me was half an inch off the bottom to get rid of the tatty ends, once a year by my mum.

Mostly in my pre-and early teen years it was kept under control by being put into plaits.

At night they were undone, and I would go to bed looking like Crystal Tipps from the cartoon Crystal Tipps and Alistair.

Once a week on a Sunday afternoon, I would be instructed to stick my head over the bath while my mum washed my hair with the aid of a cup.

I **always** got shampoo in my eyes. Two shampoos and then conditioner, just on the ends. No one shampoo's twice anymore, do they?

I never really understood the conditioner bit, because I always had a million knots in the **middle** of my hair. It was always a head yanking experience having my hair combed out after washing. There was generally enough hair in the comb at the end of it to make a mohair coat. Then it was at least 30 minutes with the hair dryer on full blast to get it to the merely damp stage.

I had a **lot** of hair. By normal standards, it was a huge amount. It was just in the normal places, I didn't have a hairy forehead or anything, but it was tightly packed in. Like good quality bedsheets, 1,000 threads per square inch.

Long luscious locks were not fun to maintain. I hated swimming lessons at school. Every other girl put her hair in one of those godawful rubber swimming hats, so easily. Straight on their head and just a bit of tucking in of the side bits. Done. And most importantly, their head shape stayed in a generally head shaped shape.

I had two huge long plaits that had to be put on top of my head like Heidi and then the cap wriggled, pulled and yanked down over them. The ends of the plaits then needed tucking round my hair line.

The result was a stupid Ferengi shaped head, under an over stretched flowery swimming cap.

I was *always* last out the changing rooms and into the pool because it took so sodding long, and I was *always* the butt of fake screaming "argh! Miss! it's a Martian in our swimming lesson!". Bloody kids.

Swimming lesson complete, the swimming cap had never done its job (unless its job was to pull a thousand hairs out of the previously neat plaits, and get my hair soaking wet) and I had to spend 30 minutes drying my hair. Always the last one out. Never with properly dry hair.

Anyway, my hair is much shorter now. And being post-menopausal, much *much* thinner.

I can practically dry my hair with the air circulation created from walking from the bathroom to my dressing table. But, even with it already being mostly dry practically immediately, it still needs a good 15 minutes of styling. Every day. *Au naturel* is very much the electric shock look.

So broken hair dryer. I thought about treating myself to a Dyson hair dryer. My eldest sister has one, so I called her up. She said she wouldn't be without it. Right, good enough for me. Off I drove to PC World/Currys.

I *hate* shopping by myself. I'd **always** shop with ODFOP. Now my life is *sans* ODFOP, if I want something today that can't be ordered on Amazon

Prime, I need to go and look at it in **public**, in an *actual* shop. By myself. Bollocks.

I parked up and sat there in the car park. Right, deep breath, no messing about.

I got out, slammed the car door, strode into the shop and straight over to the Dyson hairdryer display. I had a purpose. I picked up the demonstration model ultra-confidently. I switched in on. I turned it up. I changed the heat setting. I changed it back.

Oh fuck. Now what?

Suddenly I felt awfully self-conscious. I had marched over like I had important owl shit to do, and now I had tested it like I was *challenging* it to be amazing.

It was just a hairdryer. A drier of hair. Who marches over to a hairdryer and *tests* it?

I was an idiot. What was it going to do other than blow out warm air? Blow out rainbow coloured streams of air with sparkles?

I lost my pretend confidence and panicked.

I looked around without *actually* looking around and saw that no one was smirking at me. Thank God. I put it down and quietly slunk off to the other side of the store. I consciously tried not to slink, but I think it did. I felt shifty and self-conscious. I tried to look as though I had purposefully looked at one thing, and now I was going to look at *the* **other** thing I came in here to look at.

Now what *was* that? I found myself in Laptops. Trying to look like I had certain things I wanted to check about laptops, I put my car keys down and typed on a few.

I wanted to give the air of having researched several laptops, I was now coming to see which one I actually liked the feel of, face to face as it were.

In truth, I just wanted to get out of the bloody shop. I didn't want a Dyson hairdryer. I didn't want a new laptop. I also didn't want to look like an idiot who strode into the shop like she knew what she wanted, turned a hairdryer on and then didn't buy it - because what? Because it *didn't blow like I thought it would*?

I suspected that every internal video surveillance camera was trained on me - I must've looked *so* suspicious. Even **I** would have stopped me at the door.

A very smiley 12-year-old shop assistant came up and asked if I needed any help. I was caught.

"no thank you - I've just come from home to tap on some keyboards for no reason at all, but I'm really looking for a hairdryer"

Nope.

Instead I said "thank you very much, I am looking at a new laptop and I'm not sure which one is right for me. Could you help?"

She said she would be delighted to help me and then she fired a million questions that I was completely unprepared for

What was I going to use it for? was I going to play games on it? play Netflix? use it for work? Did I want a tablet? a Solid State or a hard drive? What about memory? what would I be storing on it? or would everything be cloud based?

Shitbags. I said I wrote a blog and I wanted something with battery life and lighter, and I'd also use it for my business in the future. "Great. What make of laptop do you have now?" I DON'T KNOW!!!! It's a big black brick.... I think I said it was a Dell - I don't even know if Dell still exists. Like Wang computer systems. What about Amstrad? Anyway, I think I said, "it's an old Dell". She didn't laugh or order me out of the shop for lying so I think I got away with it.

I did get caught out once, being put on the spot and lying out of sheer panic. I was being interviewed and my CV didn't have any school qualifications on - I assumed since it had been a long time since I had been at school it was irrelevant - anyway, it was a panel interview and one person asked me what qualifications I had from school. I went through my O

Levels, and the man said, "what about A levels?" The truth is I didn't do any A levels. I panicked and lied.

I said I had a Woodwork A Level.

God knows why. I did do Woodwork at O level, but there ISN'T a woodwork A Level. Why didn't I just say English Literature and Maths like any normal idiot. The man said "Woodwork A level? I didn't know there was such a thing", "oh yes, there is" I replied. The interview carried on and he got his mobile phone out and very obviously started googling it. He interrupted a colleague mid question "it says here, there is no woodwork A Level".

They all just looked at me. I said I must've been mistaken, and it was a very long time ago. I was beetroot coloured and had a blotchy neck. The interview finished pretty quickly after that.

Anyway, the 12-year-old IT Wizz kid was showing me round lots of laptops, telling me lots of things I didn't understand. She was looking me straight in the eyes and she just must've known I didn't have a Scooby about solid state verses Hard drive. She said "Oh, I know what would be perfect for you! We have one here on clearance price. Only one left. Very high spec. It's got blah de blah as well as dual womftyhumfs and you can also use it as a tablet. It's brilliant, I nearly bought it myself, but it didn't have a splurdeetwiddle, which you need for fast computer games - you won't need that for your blog or business. Top of the range needlewops as well. It really is a top machine. You will love it!

You will love it. There it is - that command. It's just so powerful. I'm trained in hypnosis, and I know that it's a powerful sales tool.

Which is why I left the shop.

With a new laptop. And no hairdryer.

I've ordered a hairdryer from Amazon Prime to arrive tomorrow.

I am never going shopping alone again.

XVII. Holidays Past – Iceland

What with the new laptop and everything, I've been uploading things to the "cloud" and generally having a tidy up of my e-life.

I booked 30 minutes today with another 12-year-old at PC World, for him to show me how to use the new laptop.

Laptops. They're not just a posh typewriter anymore, they're your new television, sketch pad, photo album, newspaper, diary, book, Filofax, set of encyclopaedias', camera, post box, and general window to the world.

His name was Chris. He was actually possibly 13, as he had wispy bits of ginger facial hair, and oh my fucking God - *soooo* much aftershave. The air shimmered around him. Not a good aftershave either. One of those my-first-aftershave types, like Lynx. My nostrils wanted to pull up the drawbridge and hermetically seal the edges, but my mouth didn't want to ingest it either. It was inescapable.

Eyes stinging slightly, and trying to breathe through my ears, I told him I had written a list of things I needed to know how to do. I showed him my bit of paper. He let out a chuckle as he read them. "So, what do you want to do with the other 25 minutes of your time?" he said, a little *too* smugly. I thought I would get through half of them and then have to book another half an hour, to finish off my list.

Four minutes later, I had ticked everything off my list and we were looking at each other.

Of course, I had no idea **how** he did what he did, but according to him, I never needed to look for these things again as he had installed them and put them somewhere clever.

Smuggy McSmugface.

"So" he said "wanna learn some cool stuff?"

"Yes, I bloomin' do!" I said, very excited. I had brought a pen and paper to write stuff down and so I leaned forward and poised my pen.

"you don't need that - just record it on your phone".

"Oh, bloody hell, I'd never be able to find it again. Please let me just write it down?"

"ok, do both" he said and with that he picked up my mobile and a micro-nano-second later it was flashing a red dot to say it was recording.

I leaned in to him and said quietly "you're very impressive. Do you, um, do *private lessons?*" Oh Fuck. that *looked* **and** *came* out completely wrong.

He flushed up and looked away. I couldn't say "oh! that came out wrong" because that would just make it worse, like I was a middle-aged man dressing in the latest teenage fashion, looking ridiculous, leering while making some lewd know-what-I-mean Monty Python nudge-nudge comment.

"Um, no. I have thought about it though - I just need to get organised".

"right-ho" I said, learning back in my chair trying to look as casual and as disinterested as I could possibly manage. "there are lots of older people out there that don't have a clue how to use their equipment properly, you could make a fortune". Oh FFS. Just shut up woman.

He moved his chair slightly away and squirmed uncomfortably.

I wanted to get up and walk out, leaving my laptop there in the aftershave fog and just never, ever go back.

I did however, want to learn some cool things so, trying to save the situation I said "I am a technical idiot. Use small words and move your hands slowly so I can see what you're doing and show me some whizzy things on this laptop".

Back on safe ground, he zipped and clicked, downloaded and moved and created so many things.

The problem was, as I was watching him, I was just going over in my head how I'd made a total dick of myself and he probably thought I was desperate dried up old spinster. So, although I was nodding, none of it was going in. I smiled and periodically said "brilliant" and "wow, amazing" but I couldn't tell you the first thing about what he showed me. The recording, dear reader, is full of "you click this, and download this, then click and drag that over here, and then open another window and paste in that format and it's done!" Nothing makes any sense.

My phone smells of bloody Lynx though.

Anyhow, he told me about storing photos "in the cloud" and not on the computer. SO, when I came home, I opened up my photos and started uploading them. I have either shared them with the whole world, or they are in a never-to-be-seen-again file.

It was nice looking through them though. There was several years of holidays ODFOP and I had taken, and they got me reminiscing and feeling a little sad.

What do you do with photos of holidays when you split up from someone?

I've always hated having my photo taken, so I have all the photos of our holidays and mostly they are of ODFOP or animals I have fed, rescued, or stopped to pet.

I didn't have any photos of it, but it got me thinking about our trip to Iceland. We went particularly to see the Aurora Borealis (we didn't see it). I **loved** Iceland. But fuck me, it's a *whole other level* of cold there.

I know there is a clue in the name of the country, but we had been to Finland many years before (again to try and see the Aurora Borealis - we didn't...) and I know that ODFOP's moustache froze then, but I was always slightly *too warm*.

So here is the thing about me. I am **always** hot. **Always**. I haven't worn a coat in maybe 15 years. Or if I have, I've end up carrying it.

Pre-menopause I was hot, perimenopause I was white shimmering nuclear hot, and post-menopause, I am probably most comfortable at 30 degrees cooler than anyone else is. Centigrade, none of this Fahrenheit nonsense.

I put it down to being large. Fat cells are like storage cells. I think I store heat *very* effectively. I *radiate* heat.

People comment if they sit down in a seat I have just got up from, because it's **hot** *like a car seat heater hot*, not just warm. I always have hot hands, hot feet and legs in bed and I can't sleep with more than a sheet over me and the window open.

In the summer, when it's hot and no-one can sleep? ODFOP has to be in another room because it's like sleeping next to a full-on radiator. And **I am** that radiator. I will often shower in cold water and just lie in front of the fan. But the sheets will dry in a matter of moments and there are no cold bits left.

If you stuck me in a cold bath and left me there long enough, the bath water would warm up so as to have gentle steam rising off it.

Bloody hell, I am a sous vide.

Anyway, safe in the knowledge that I was always slightly too hot in Finland (and it got down to minus 25), I confidently packed for Iceland. The temperature said it averaged at freezing at that time of year. Just zero? Bloody t-shirt weather! Four-day trip with tours of the geezers, waterfalls, the crack where Iceland is pulling itself apart on separate tectonic plates, and a couple of aurora borealis trips. Perfect. I took a large knit poncho, more for decoration than anything and one thermal vest, one fleece and some long sleeve cotton tops. I had jeans, socks and practical boots because I knew we would be walking. ODFOP packed thermal leggings, thermal long sleeve tops, thin jumpers and thick jumpers, an ex-Russian Military parka that he bought for Finland, thermal socks, two pairs of gloves, a thermal hat, a woollen hat and goggle sunglasses. He said I should take a hat, so I took a hat that was more of a Fascinator than a keep-your-head-warm hat.

The poncho was that kind of knitted-with-your-arms instead of small knitting needles, knit, big wool with lots of big holes. I had to wear it travelling to Iceland as it wouldn't fit in my suitcase.

I was **roasting**.

Probably in the early stages of perimenopause, I felt like a global warming event all by myself. I had overdone it. I should have just taken a fleece, I *knew* it.

Getting off the plane was under a covered walkway - I couldn't wait to get outside and cool off. I was dripping with sweat. Out of the airport and straight into a coach - a heated coach.

I was miserable.

Skinny feckers with their tight little puffa jackets done right up, two scarves, two hats, skiing gloves, salopettes and big snow boots and they were rubbing their hands together to keep warm as they got on the coach. "Ooooh, close the door!" they would all cry when the driver opened it to let new people on.

I wanted to **kill them**.

I was sitting as close to the door as possible, drinking in the cool air for the brief moment it was allowed in. If I'd had my wits about me I would've tied myself to the roof for the journey to the hotel.

The **heated** hotel.

By the time we were dropped off at our hotel I was near breaking point. I ran/wept/crawled to the hotel

197

room and switched the frigging heating off as soon as I got in there, opened the windows and stripped off.

I had a cool shower and lay on the bed on a towel and gently steamed. ODFOP was sat there with his stupid parka and gloves still on.

He looked at me.

"Do we **have** to?" I whined.

"It is **normal** for this country" he said, as he got up and closed the window.

Bollocks.

He conceded to not having the heating on, but when he took his gloves off, his hands were *cold*. WTF? He took his boots and two pairs of socks off and his **feet** were cold. Just *crazy*. Like two people trying to stave off with hypothermia, we stripped off and got into bed, and spooned.

I delighted in him tucking his cold feet into my bended knees - luxury! His cold hands fitted perfectly under my huge boobs.

Within minutes he was toasty, and I was desperately trying to find a cold bit of his skin to absorb. But there was none. At that moment, spooning became *smothering*. I was over-heating! Cue, me unwrapping myself from romantic spooning at lightning speed, and throwing off the covers. ODFOP, used to this, turned over and wrapped himself in the double duvet and fell immediately asleep.

How does he do that? From lying in bed talking, to finishing the conversation to him gently snoring, is *never* more than 5 breaths. NEVERRRRRRR. How does he switch his brain off?????

I am lying there thinking about everything that we've talked about, or how I am going to deal with something tomorrow, for at least an hour and a half after we say goodnight.

ODFOP is not the only one... I have even spoken to *women* who are able to do what ODFOP does. Just switch off and go to sleep. In an un-comfy bed? No problem. A party going on down the road? Still no problem. When you are worried about something? Not an issue. Just breathe and **sleep.**

I have never had that gift. For many years pre-ODFOP and early ODFOP, the only thing I could fall asleep to was a tape recording of a massive thunder and rain storm. ODFOP got rid of the tape recorder, and that was that. We switched to Classic FM. Since the ODFOP split, I will lie there and listen to Relaxing Classics from 10.00 p.m. to 1.00 a.m. and you can bet your bottom dollar I am still listening at 1.30 a.m.

Anyway, Iceland. I was *roasting* and ODFOP's nose was cold.

Our first day trip was the following morning. We went down to breakfast to see all the skinny bitches in puffa jackets, hats and gloves etc. I came down in a long-sleeved t-shirt. People stared. Ha! more fool them, I thought. ODFOP said I should definitely take my fleece and poncho, I could always leave them on the coach. I begrudgingly conceded and went back up to the room to get them.

Off we went. In the heated-to-tropical-temperatures coach. First stop was the Gullfoss Waterfalls. I was so looking forward to this. The coach pulled in and everyone got off. I decided to leave the fleece and put on the poncho. I stepped off the bus. Hmm. a little nippier that I thought it would be, but that's always a good thing for me. I'll be fine.

The coaches were providing quite a lot of shelter, so I was to discover.... We started to walk down the path to the waterfalls. It was icy, so I was slow. ODFOP went on ahead. I said I'd catch him up.

You could hear the roar of the waterfalls, it was exciting! I cleared the last of the coaches and the wind hit me.

Holy bollocking shit, man! It was the **coldest** thing I have *ever* experienced. Every hole in my poncho was allowing this whistling, excruciating bone-freezing wind through. This wind didn't stop at skin, this wind went through you, swirled round you like a washing machine full of ice cubes and then smacked you round the face on the way out.

My face, Jesus, my face was actually FROZEN stiff. My hands were bright red and raw with cold. My stupid hat flew off. My legs in jeans, well, it was like I was naked, except my jeans were stiff.

Wind was whipping behind my sunglasses and my eyes were streaming, the tears making my cheeks sting.

Fuck the fucking waterfall. I took one photo from a distance and turned around, genuinely wondering if I was going to survive long enough to get to the gift shop, so I could die in the warm.

I slipped and slid and cursed like I had never cursed before - and I am good curser. Whole new levels of expletives bubbled up and were trying to escape from my now blue, stiff, lips. I was like a ventriloquist because my face was frozen solid, I couldn't purse my lips.

After what felt like an age, I pushed the door of the gift shop with my frozen solid, bare claw of a hand. Oh, my fucking life. I have **never** welcomed heat like I did then. My eyes were still streaming, and my mouth was a pillar box of pain.

Within 30 seconds, my ears were on **fire**.

I didn't care. I was **never** leaving the safety of that shop. I took a hat, gloves, scarf, another fleece, ear protectors and put them all on immediately. My ears were throbbing like red belisha beacons. I took the ear protectors off. People shielded their eyes from the glare. Now my nose was heating up and developing its

201

own throb. My fingers were starting to burn, but I still couldn't un-claw them.

"Would you like to buy those?" I turned around and there was a kind face smiling at me - not smirking. She had a shopping basket in her hand to offer me, but I couldn't take it from her. "um. yes please"

"come with me, and we'll sort you out" she said in a "I've seen other broken menopausal women in here before" kind of way. She added some wet wipes to my order and gestured to her face. I nodded.

I couldn't open my handbag. She took it from me and said, "May I?",

"Oh, please do" I whimpered gratefully. She took my purse out and opened for me. I managed to pick out a card and hand it to her. She carefully put a pen between my fingers and I signed a mad signature. She put the ear protectors and the wipes in a plastic bag and cut the tags off the fleece, hat, scarf and gloves. "The Ladies is just over there" she said as she gestured to her face again. "thank you so much" I said, grateful to this wonderful woman.

I staggered to the Ladies and entered. I looked in the mirror.

Sweet Jesus. My face was white and blue with mascara streaks down my cheeks, being blown to my ears half way down.

My ears were radiation red and burning. My mouth was still a pillar box, my hands unable to un-claw.

The overall effect was sort of a little bit like Heath Ledger as the Joker, but without the cute lipstick.

Everything was not just warming up, it was all starting to properly *burn*. My nose was turning deep red and starting to throb. My cheeks were turning purple, the tips of my fingers were on fire.

I managed to clean my face with my burning claws. My cheeks were roasting. I was turning into one of those red-faced monkeys. I pulled the hat down over my ears and my new fleecy scarf up over my mouth.

I still looked radioactive.

I found the courage to say, "fuck it" and I walked out of the Ladies straight into ODFOP who was angry and looking for me.

"Where the fuck did you... Jesus! what's happened to your *face*?"...

By then my mouth had defrosted and I blurted out the whole sorry story.

I've only seen ODFOP cry with laughter a handful of times. This was the first time. Every time he opened his eyes and looked at me, he would start again.

I wanted to *burn* him with my face.

I had challenged Iceland to be cold, and Iceland had laughed like a drain and froze my assets without even giving me a second glance.

Respect to Iceland.

XVIII. New Year – New Me

God (or someone who can actually help), please help me.

I have a **lot** of changes to make in my life, and bloody New Year's Day is just 2 really poor, anxious sleeps away.

It's **obviously** the perfect time to start creating the new me - but *where the hell do I start?* Do I begin alphabetically? By size of change required? Start easy and *then* tackle the big shit? Or start with the tough ones and then everything else will be a breeze?

I am a bombsite. My life is a bombsite. The road to bombshell is long, all uphill, and full of landmines of temptation, and potholes of comfort.

This is a *big job* for one person to take on.

I know what Bombshell-me looks like.

- I have **one** chin.
- I have a top lip, but I don't look like a trout pout.

- I have no frown lines.
- I have good skin.
- I can wear an underwired bra all day without wanting to commit murder (or take it off on the bus/train/taxi/ladies' toilet at work).
- I will be able to wear clothes that **have a waistband**, and it won't just scrunch up and leave a red line on my stomach.
- Medium heels won't feel like my toes are pushed into a point by a 50-tonne weight.
- I will wake fully refreshed in the morning.
- I will be intelligent and witty and will be able to go out with friends without feeling the need to shower them with £50 notes or get humongously hammered, or both.
- I will take, and if not *enjoy*, not *loathe*, regular exercise.
- I will have a *hairstyle*. Oh God, I would **love** to have a hairstyle. I can go into any hairdressers with a picture of the hair I want, and the very best I come out with, is just shorter hair.
- I will have positive male attention from someone I consider to be out of my league (anyone above Quasimodo).

It's all a big ask from a big ass.

In order to get anywhere close to that, I need to do practically everything I am doing now, differently.

I am struggling already with the wanting to give up before I've started.

These are the things I need to do in order to give myself any chance of success.

I do realise that once these things are down on paper and "out there" it will be harder to give in, because I really don't want to be a wuss in front of you, my precious, solitary reader.

So, would you like instead to hear about the time I jumped naked off the boat and couldn't get myself back in? It's the second time that I've seen ODFOP cry with laughter and be totally unable to fucking help me get back in the boat... The first rung of the stupid ladder back into the boat was by my ear. Over an hour it took me. I genuinely thought ODFOP was going to have to tow me to a beach and leave me there.

No? Perhaps another time.

Right, here goes.

Number one. Stop drinking wine for three months. Oh Jesus. I don't know if I can. Chablis is to me, is what Torvill is to Dean. Abbott is to Costello. Cagney to Lacey. Starsky to Hutch. Fred to Ginger.

We've gone through *so much* together. Much of it is, of course, just a vague gnawing feeling in my gut, that sense that I've done something stupid but can't quite remember what it is. We've shared *countless* evenings like that.

My memories of these events tend to be kept with other people, and they remind me through tears of laughter, the next time that we are getting together - and then I do it again.

Waaay too many stories of shame to list here, but some drunken events may pepper this blog.

It is entirely possible that my local purveyors of vegan wine will go bust during these three, endlessly long, barren, devoid of all human comfort, months.

The truth is, I comfort drink. And I sometimes need *a lot* of comforting. I don't know when to stop.

Basically, what goes through my head with each sip is "I must say, this wine is making me want to have more wine".

Jeez, I did promise to be honest in this blog. Ok, ok, I don't sip, ever. I quaff.

Did you know that a bottle of white wine is the equivalent number of calories of 2/3rds of a jam and cream filled Victoria Sponge? Family sized cake. A Victoria Sponge is practically all eggs, butter and sugar.

There are many *many* times when I have consumed one and a third cakes worth in an evening. Yes, I know that one and a third cake is two bottles.

What body can take that, and not end up looking like a blubbery ball?

Not mine, apparently.

I came to alcohol relatively late in life. I was always the driver in the group, drinking Britvic's Bitter Lemon or Diet Coke. I just didn't like the *taste* of alcohol. I went through a brief stint of Pernod and black in my teens, but one day it was just too sickly sweet I just couldn't ever drink it again.

My mum never drunk, but my dad - well he drunk *a lot*. Not at home, unless they were entertaining, but out socialising, mostly wining and dining people as part of his job. Well, he made wining and dining a BIG part of his job.

when I was 23, I went to Australia to travel round a bit.

I ended up in a tiny town in the outback of Western Australia, in love with a sheep farmer called Scratch. I had never smoked weed and didn't drink alcohol, so I was perfect for Scratch. I was perfect, because I could be trusted to go to his secret marijuana growing site in a corner of one of his fields, and water and feed the plants. I was never going to steal any of it. I would also be trusted not to drink his "tinnie" of Emu when he went for a "slash" when in the pub. He was a delight.

I was living with a friend of mine in a bungalow on the outskirts of town with about 12 sheep shearers who were there for the "season".

Oh, My Good God.

Every night was party night. I have no idea how they survived. They would go to bed at about 2.00 a.m. totally off their heads, and then get up at 5.00 a.m. shear sheep all day, come home, get showered, go for "tea" at the Roadhouse and then straight to the pub. When the pub closed, they would bring home as much Emu beer as they could carry, and the stereo went on and we'd do it all over again.

My friend and I slept most of the day while they were out, just to recover.

There was Duncan, who looked like he was in ZZ Top, Rolly, Dwayne, Pumpkin, Yot, and several others who were just a blur of partying animals. Scratch used to take me round his farm in his Ute, with his dog Yotty in the back.

He was a tough bastard. A real outback born and bred farmer. He never went anywhere without a gun. He had several.

I saw my first ever Kangaroo with Scratch. I was so excited. He drove the Ute up close to it and leaned back so I could take some photos.

He then shot it.

He took my camera out of my shocked hands and took some photos of the first dead kangaroo I'd ever seen.

That was Scratch.

The first time I stayed over at his house and we'd been up all night having amazing sex, we'd just fallen asleep and the Gallah's landed in the trees outside and were making early morning Gallah noises.

He got out of bed, went to the trees and shot the birds. They were the first Gallah's I'd ever seen close-up. Beautiful pink and grey cockatoos. Now dead.

It was never going to work between us. But, the people-pleasing force was strong, and I was going to "help him see the error of his ways" and make him worth loving.

Anyway, I am digressing with all these distressing, animal killing memories.

It was time for the marijuana to be harvested and so Scratch took me to his secret growing fields. We cut all the plants down and loaded them into two sacks. We then took them to the shearers house where under my guard, they were dried out slowly in the oven.

The shearers were pacing like they were expecting a baby.

Eventually it was dry enough, and the Mother of All Parties started. Everyone was completely stoned but having a great time. It was at that party that they got hold of my camera and all the shearers took a picture of their penises.

This was 1989, and you had to send your film off to be developed. They also did not send you back any rude photos. No-one told me about the penis pictures, I didn't think I'd used all my photos up, but hey ho, apparently, I had.

When the photos came back everyone was so excited to look at them. This was odd, normally they couldn't give a stuff. There was a handwritten note in the packet that said that they were disgusted that I had sent this reel in to be developed and I was lucky that they didn't give the police my address. The note was pinned up in the house for months. The funny thing was that one cock shot got through. He was then known as Odd Cock, because the developers clearly didn't recognise his penis as, a penis.

Anyhow, they all decided in their deeply stoned state, that it would be hilarious to see what I was like stoned. They danced round me in a circle while chanting for me to "draw deep" on this joint. I thought I may as well try it, as I did feel a little bit left out being the only one not stoned, and they were all having such a good time. What's the harm in trying it once?

I had one drag on this foot long, pure marijuana joint. Within less than a minute I couldn't speak. My tongue felt so thick, it completely filled my mouth and my head and body. My head spun, and I couldn't open my mouth because my tongue was going to spill out everywhere, and I wouldn't be able to fit it back in. The shearers started a conga around me and I sat there, unable to move.

I was still sat there 4 hours later. Scratch had tried to take me back to his house, but I couldn't move. Shearers were asleep around me on the kitchen floor and I was sat at this plastic kitchen table just staring at the wall as it moved like a snake in front of me.

It took me three days to get back to normal. "Who's got my stash? Kate is it you again?" was the running joke. They would plant it in my pockets, in my bed, in the fridge behind my diet coke. "Jesus Kate - you need to lay off this stuff a little" and then they'd crack up and light another joint.

At one of the parties, a Mauri shearer called Jake, the scariest fecker you could ever hope to not meet, offered me a drink of Bundaberg rum.

I'd never had it before and I didn't want it, but no one ever said "no" to Jake. So, I tried it. And I *loved* it.

Bundaberg and coke were my new thing. Every party, which was every night, and I was drinking "bundy and coke". I built up an admirable tolerance for it, and an enjoyment of being slightly pissed with the shearers and Scratch and my mate from home.

Some of the best times I have ever had, I had in that tiny town of Newdegate, Western Australia with bundy and coke as my companion.

No Bundaberg in the UK, but an enjoyment in getting slightly trollied, let to experimentation with booze and a settlement on Chablis as my poison of choice.

From being like my mum, much to her disappoint, I started to be more like my dad...The rest, as they say, is history.

A 28-year relationship with chilled white wine. I have given many of my friend's stories to tell at dinner parties, and I have paid handsomely for a weight gain that has pushed me so far into the Morbidly Obese category that I am almost in a new category of my own.

So, no wine for three months. From Monday. Shitbags, it's already Saturday night now....

Secondly. I need to get fit. Since getting together with ODFOP, I have become sloth-like. I have been in the Fitness Protection Programme. We both enjoy and glass or 10 of wine, and he liked my cooking.

In my school days I used to be a gymnast. A good one too. Every lunch time was spent in the gymnasium or on the trampoline.

Most nights after school were at gymnastics clubs.

I could do the splits all three ways, I could do forward and backward walk-overs and a back-flip from standing. I could do a somersault at the end of a long tumble of back flips and I could do a backward

214

walkover on the beam. I could also do a double backward somersault on the trampoline.

I was as bendy as a U-bend. And I totally took it for granted. I couldn't understand all my stiff friends who couldn't leap frog the horse, do a cartwheel, or do a somersault off the end of the beam - what were they scared of? I was fearless and had no idea that this would ever end.

Then I left school and I just didn't have access to it all. It stopped right then. I used to go to the local sports centre and do a bit of trampolining, but boys came along, and I was distracted, so it all just came to a grinding halt.

Now, I take two goes to get off the sofa.

So, I am joining Shapers. A women's only gym about half a mile away. I have my induction on Saturday 6th January. I am going to walk there and walk back. I am going to go there every week day unless I am working late, and I am going to do half an hour of exercise. This time, would be my normal sitting on the sofa drinking wine time, so it is better to be distracted doing something healthy.

I am going to walk from the train station to work, every day that I go into London for work. It is a mile.

I am going to walk from the train station to home. It is just over half a mile.

215

I am going to find a yoga class and go to yoga, fully aware of the fact that I am totally stiff, fat and unbendable, but the more I go, the suppler and less fat and stiff I will become.

I am going to go to bed physically tired and listen to a meditation every night to help me sleep.

Thirdly, I am going to aim to eat half a kilo of green vegetables and fruit a day.

Fourthly, I am not going to let myself slip into eating any more dairy - I hate the thought of dairy, but I find myself having some of ODFOP's butter occasionally and I loathe myself for it. **No more dairy.**

My hope is that at the end of three months, my skin will be better, I would have lost maybe 2 stone, I will not be out of breath climbing the stairs, I will be fitter, mentally stronger and more prepared for my future as a single woman in her 50's.

So dear reader, bless you for still reading. I am joining Instagram and I am going to post a picture of my feet on the scales each week, because you are watching, and you DEMAND this progress of me.

Some of my posts during this three months of purgatory, while I expiate my past demons and dreadful habits, may be just be me sobbing onto my lap top. I do hope you will bear with me.

I so want to be a bombshell. But to start that journey, I really must clear this bombsite of comforting distractions.

Holy shit-bags. You know I'm kidding, right?

XIX. It Has Begun

There are no more "next weeks", no more "oh bugger it, I'll start again tomorrows".

I am now on Instagram and Twitter. I have announced my fatness to the world and declared publicly that I will do lots of very positive things in order to rid myself of it.

I am begrudgingly learning about using hashtags. I don't really understand them, but I do know I don't like them.

I have a friend who posts on Facebook with regular angry rants about how "they" aren't taking proper action to rid this country of terrorists, criminals, teenagers, queue jumpers, Leave voters or vegans. He always ends these rants with #sadforhumanity. It makes my nostrils flare.

30 years ago, he would have been writing to the Times daily "Sir, am I the *only* person to have noticed that our policeman no longer doff their helmets when a

gentleman walks past? I am outraged that we, the tax payer, who pay their wages..."

I suppose, if I *have* to be fair about it, my nostril flaring makes me as bigoted and as ignorant as I think some of his rants are. I know he is coming from a good place. I am not the font of all knowledge and wisdom by any means, and don't have the answers to his "why oh why in this day and age..." pieces, but then, nor does he. But the #sadforhumanity to me, seems like he's portraying himself as a wise superhero, who has vowed not to get involved in human life, but *if only* he were allowed 10 minutes with the right people, he could sort it all out for us, simple fools.

It's also possible that I am reading too much into 14 letters and a hashtag.

I don't really know why the hashtag is the focus of my dislike. It's an innocent enough symbol. Right, I am determined to give the hashtag a break. Prove me wrong hashtag, show me the good that you do... #showmewhatyouvegothashtag.

Maybe it is his **anger** that gets my goat. It is entirely possible, as someone who has perfected the art of seeing the other persons side *at all costs*, that I am **jealous** of his commitment to one viewpoint, despite there being many other points to consider on the subject.

There is not much I am 100% certain of in life. And even when I am, some bastard generally comes along

219

and tips over that little pebble of security and throws in another "valid" view.

A good example is trophy hunting. I feel disgusted and horrified when I see a post on Facebook or in the news with a person crouched next to a majestic murdered animal, and they are smiling like they're brave.

See? Anger is seeping out of me right now, even just *thinking* about a hypothetical trophy hunter.

I was confident, and self-assured in my feelings about trophy hunting, and I would happily comment on the posts with bile ridden venom, aimed at said smiling tosspot, along the lines of wanting them to die horrible and painful deaths for what they've done. I know. Proper venomous hate speech.

Yet, a very nice, intelligent, friend of mine always tries to bring to the many insults and death threats that typically get added to such a post, a little balance. Of course, it gets on my nerves. I want to be right, because I FEEL right.

Did I know, for example, that most of the animal reserves in Africa are paid for by trophy hunters? I did not know that. But even if that *is* the case, I **still** want to stamp on their heads. The trophy hunters apparently pay such large sums to stalk and shoot a "big game" animal, that it pays for all the conservation and the anti-poaching guards - the whole kit and caboodle.

These bastard tossknobs, sorry Trophy Hunters, do not get to choose which animal they can shoot. It is one that is considered to be "surplus to requirements" and they are pretty much rounded up and put in front of these wankbreath fucktards, who are then handed a high-powered rifle.

So my educating friend puts to me - would you rather have no conservation, no anti-poaching police and lots of animals being killed by poachers in very inhumane ways (humane killing - that's the **biggest** oxymoron ever, muttermuttermutter) or much less poaching, safer animals with proper breeding programmes that are no longer endangered, and the odd old, spare lion shot humanely (grrr) in a controlled environment?

Obviously, with Lalala in control, I would like everyone to just be a lot kinder to each other and their fellow sentient beings and not feel the need or even have the capability to do harm to anyone or anything else.

Apparently, that's not an option because cruel, ignorant fuck trumpets abound, and we can't just put them all in a big room with a load of guns and let nature take its course. Don't see why not - most people will get to shoot at least one thing dead muttermutter....

So, there are never just two sides to an argument, debate or fact. In fact, there are very few actual bona fide, can't- argue-with-them, *facts* out there. It's pretty much up to every individual's opinion or belief. Even the Law of Physics. Scotty repeatedly shouted, *"I just*

221

cannae do it Captain, you cannae deny the laws of physics" and the Star Ship Enterprise *never did* blow up, and they *always* got out of their scrapes.... #lawsofphysicsarenotsomuchlawsreallyarethey?

In summary, I think one thing is abundantly clear, I am obviously a little unhappy about being on a diet and exercise plan that I can't just wriggle out of. Blimey, look at that rant! I was even ranting about ranting!

That was a Rantasorus of the rant species. #rantasorusrant

And breathe.

I think I need some fruit for dinner. Maybe some grapes, or just grape juice, fermented grape juice perhaps - ok, maybe I just need wine for dinner. #liquiddinner

Here I am day 3 of my at least 365-day plan to get to the new improved, half the woman I am now, me and I've already threatened trophy hunters, called a friend bigoted and ignorant, another friend annoying, and tapped **very** hard on my brand-new keyboard. #totesawks

I've got this.

I am breathing in and breathing out. I am going to calmly get up, walk slowly to the kitchen and heat up my parsnip soup.

No wine shall pass my bitter, pinched lips tonight. #muttermuttermutter

XX. The "C" Word

Not **that** C word. I do have *some* class. The **other** one.

Children.

I am the youngest child and there is 16 years between me and my eldest sister. My eldest niece Tortie, is just four years younger than me, but four light years ahead in intelligence. That's *Doctor* Tortie, to you and I....

I grew up with my brother and sisters having children, and me getting to babysit, and in the case of my brother who is only a few years older than me, having his three kids to stay over for weekends.

I loved it.

I have always been enthralled by how people think and *why* they think **what** they think, and children are just so open and unguarded. It's been a privilege to watch them develop and grow, while not having to be worried about the, well, daily maintenance, and upkeep of actually *owning* a child...

My mum and both my sisters married young (19, 19 & 21) and they all had children pretty much immediately, ergo I genuinely thought I was supposed to have a couple of years of working in a job (not career), find someone, get married, stop working and look after my husband and children.

That was it. That was success. I had three happy role models to look to. It's what I **wanted**. I couldn't *wait* for it to happen to me.

I stayed on to the 6th form at school and then I didn't know what to do.

I know! I like kids, I'll train as a Nursery Nurse. Not a Norland Nanny, just your average nursery assistant or standard nanny.

I went to Southwark College and did 2 years with one week on a placement at a nursery or school and one week in college. I loved every second of it. I loved the placements, I loved the kids, I loved what I was learning. This was going to be soooo handy for when I had children. I was really going to be able to produce little balanced, intelligent, ambitious and capable people.

My teens came and went,

Then so did my twenties...

No husband, no children. Failure.

Of course, you know about my teens and 20's. My pre-ODFOP years. I was just desperate to find someone who wanted to stay until *breakfast*, never mind wanted to have *children* with me.

Just before I married Akram, I was sitting reading those magazines that you picked up on the way into work on a Monday morning, Ms London or None to Five or another one of those ilk. Lots of jobs for PA's in London and a bit about fashion.

There was this advert asking for women to consider donating their eggs to couples who couldn't have their own children....

Oh yes. <Lipstick Taser!!> My people-pleasing radar was flashing, and the sirens were going off in my head. I could also help create a life, satisfying my own ticking body clock. *How* **marvellous**.

I signed up straight away.

I didn't know this until afterwards, but they normally only accept people that have had their own children, and **not** childless fruit loops who want to manically take over the life problems of anyone who may (or may not) give them eye contact...

It turns out they were desperate, as I don't think I was even asked if I'd had my own children or why I wanted to do it...

I had the medical checks and was deemed to be medically, if not mentally, fit to donate eggs.

I was told that two couples would be getting my eggs. The nurses asked to write a note to the couples.

Something anonymous that didn't identify me but told them a bit about me.

I did a little story about there being a mix up at the egg factory, and I accidentally got their eggs - so this was restoring karmic order. I told them that I sometimes felt I didn't belong on this planet, so if their child developed antennae, then I was probably right.

The doctor was really happy with it and asked me to write an article on my experience as an egg donator, so they could use to encourage other people to do it. My first published article!

I never saw it anywhere though.

I had to take lots of pills and inject myself once a day with a hormone that made my eggs ripen at the same time. Several checks at the hospital (that was the first time I discovered *internal* ultrasound - **that** was a shock!) and then I was ripe for the plucking.

When I arrived at the hospital I was whisked into a separate waiting room with no window. People coming in and out were very careful to make sure the door was shut as quickly as possible. It didn't even dawn on me why, and then one of the nurses said. The couples had to be there at the same time, so they could (cough) jizz into a cup and mix it up with my eggs as soon as possible.

They were **here**. Suddenly they became actual *people* to me.

The corridor was cleared, and I was whisked upstairs to a medical room. I got changed and was sitting on the bed with the gown on wondering what was going to happen next, and this massive bunch of flowers walked in. It was absolutely the most beautiful bouquet I had ever *seen,* let alone **received**. One of the couples had brought them for me and it had the most amazing thank you note attached to them.

I was overwhelmed, overcome, and promptly burst in tears. I so wanted to hug them for making me feel **special**.

A nurse was despatched by the doctor, who I think was a little freaked by my tears, and she sat on the bed and fed me tissues, patted me on the knee and told me it was the hormones.

I had just recovered my composure when another nurse came in with a card. They'd had to open it because the couple may have put their names in it or contact details and indeed, the woman who had written it had accidentally put her husband's first name in the card so it was blocked out with black marker pen.

It was beautiful.

She knew that I was the right person to help them, she couldn't tell me how much this meant to them, they had been struggling for several years and they were so excited they neither of them had slept since they were given my note.

Cue more bawling from me.

I don't think I had even considered them as people in much detail throughout this little escapade of mine - not as *real people*, struggling, exhausted, desperate people whose all-consuming focus was for her to get pregnant and carry their child. I never considered their struggles or their emotions. To be perfectly honest, I was probably jealous that she had someone that loved her enough to want to have children with her and that was that. My own self-centred little world.

These flowers and cards had thrown me right out of my little ignorant world and suddenly I *desperately* wanted everything to go smoothly for these couples, I **needed** to not disappoint them. They had made *me* feel *special.*

I was walked, sobbing in an open arse gown and socks, down to theatre. The anaesthetist was annoyed that I was snotty as I would be having a tube down my throat and snottiness complicated it. I had to sit on the operating table and blow my nose repeatedly in front of half a dozen people until he was satisfied.... I felt like a small child being told off for not brushing my teeth properly.

Legs in stirrups, the screen with the camerascope on facing me, I started to ask if I could watch it happen, and then I was in recovery waking up.

I was really pissed off that I'd missed it all.

How many eggs did they get? was the first thing I asked. 19 said the nurse. Very impressive she said. My chest swelled with pride. I was a high producer...

Wheeled up back to the room, I saw the flowers and started sobbing again. I was given a chicken sandwich and a cup of disgusting tea and left to it. After half an hour they came and took my blood pressure and then disappeared again. I got dressed and got ready to go. I walked out of the room and the nurse came running and said I couldn't go yet because the couples were downstairs and were just about to leave. I looked out of the window, from five floors up, at the exit, but couldn't catch sight of them.

Half an hour later I was allowed out and I got the train home.

I was on the train **with flowers**. Something I had *always* wanted to happen to me - but it was a week day and about 3.00 p.m. so no one was really there to see it. Bugger. I should've waited until rush hour.

I was told I could contact them in a month or so and they would be able to tell me if any of the eggs had resulted in a fertilised egg that could be transplanted.

After the first week I noticed that I was getting more and more bloated. My stomach was a round ball (back when it wasn't that shape through too much wine and cake). I went to the doctor and he sent me straight to hospital. I wish I could remember the name of what they said was wrong with me, I vaguely recollect it sounded like elephantiasis...I basically had ovaries that were the size of basket balls and my body was storing fluid around them. I had to pee in a measuring jug and write down every liquid that went in, and out.

The ward was a gynaecological ward, and was full of women having hysterectomies, medical abortions, tubes tied etc. Everyone was in tears. It was miserable.

They let me out after about 5 days of peeing in a jug and my elephant ovaries had calmed down.

I called the hospital after a month and asked how it had all gone. 11 eggs had fertilised. Seven for one couple and four for the other couple. They'd both had three eggs transplanted into them and that was all they could tell me. well done me.

I told them about my hospital stay and the doctor went potty. He said he could've given me an injection that would've cured that in a few hours. What? And miss 5 days in a ward with sobbing women? I wouldn't have missed that for the world...

Anyway, who knows what happened. Well, some people do I suppose. I hope it worked.

I don't know how the subject came up, but I told ODFOP about the egg donation shortly after we got together.

He had cried. He said it was the kindest thing he'd ever heard. Well, blow me, I liked that! So, of course, I did it again. 35 was the normal upper age limit and I was 36, but they were desperate, and I had done it before, so they were delighted to have me back.

ODFOP gave me the injections and came with me to the hospital. I didn't get cards or flowers this time, but I didn't even notice. I had something better, **I had a man who loved me.**

21 eggs that time - back of the net! Three sets of couples. I don't even remember ringing up to find out what happened that time. I was happy and in love.

So anyway, children for me. ODFOP had spent the year that we spent on opposite couches saying that he hadn't wanted children, but his first wife wanted one, so they had one. He never thought he could be a good father because he had a crappy role model and so just wanted to really give the whole fatherhood thing the go-by.

Once they split, his son came and stayed with us a few times, but it got so awful with his ex-wife saying I had split them up and his son calling me terrible names (and ODFOP not defending me, by the way) that he used to go to Eastbourne to visit him for the day at the weekend. That became every fortnight, and that soon became never.

With ODFOP not wanting another child, that was that. He said he would have a vasectomy and he got booked in. I went with him to the hospital and when they called his name I had a mild panic attack. I grabbed him and asked him if he was completely sure. He really didn't want to think about it some more?

He looked at me oddly and just said "no, I don't want to think about it anymore, I don't want to have any more children". He laughed at my clinging on to his arm, in an embarrassed kind of way, and unhooked me, kissed me on the forehead and said he'd be back in a while with swollen bollocks.

That was that. That was the day that I knew I was never going to have any children.

I went out of the waiting room and had a cigarette (yes, I know) in the car and cried.

Luckily, I had Lalala on my side. She packaged that ticking bomb up and double boxed it. Extra rivets and soldered, a big sign saying UNDER NO CIRCUMSTANCES TRY TO OPEN THIS BOX and she then wheel-barrowed to the edge of the cliff and chucked over. That one had to sink *right out of sight*.

It did...

I count myself as one of the lucky ones. Lalala did good.

I love my nieces and nephews. They are beautiful, handsome, successful and happy. Two of them have children of their own, and those kids, well, they are just amazing. My sisters are grannies and I love watching them with their grandchildren. There is a special bond there that is just so all consuming.

My niece, Banana, is expecting her second child in a few weeks' time.

I remember this beautiful little 3-year-old toddler, 30 odd years ago, who had an infectious giggle and big beautiful eyes, sitting on her Granny's knee at the kitchen table, saying "tell me again" over and over. My mum would smile and tell again the story of when she was born and how beautiful and special she was.

Now she is an amazing mum with a beautiful, funny, confident, 3-year-old treasure of her own - who sings Bruno Mars songs word-for-word into a karaoke microphone, while she has her eyes shut, her head back, and her arms out as she dances like no one is watching. Her granny, my sister, absolutely glows with love for this little being.

I am warmly welcomed into my sisters and my brothers lives, and I get all the benefits of their children that they do.

I am blessed to be an aunty. I don't need to be a mum.

XXI. This Old House

Since the first day I moved back into this house, the house I grew up in from age 13, eleven and a half years ago, I have wanted *desperately* to move **out** of it.

Not so good memories, no mum here, ODFOP and dad tormenting and bitching about each other, me wanting something that was new to *both* of us, and the house needing totally renovating, meant that I wasn't happy or comfortable here.

Some good and some bad reasons why we couldn't move, prevailed, and I was stuck here.

You may recall, after the first year or so, my father and ODFOP were at war with each other. They both expected me to be their counsellor, their verbal dumping ground and punch bag, their Squire, Knight and Second, who has sworn allegiance to only them, as well as the Mediator and Blame Taker.

If I didn't agree with either of them *vigorously enough* that what they said the other had done was truly dreadful, then I was always "sticking up for my stupid fucking father", or "protecting *that man*, over my own father, when *I knew* that he'd done it".

That was day in, day out for between eight and nine years....

My father's way of getting his own back, was to sit in the Lounge and smoke huge cigars with the door open.

It was my fault if the door wasn't shut and the house stank. When my father went to bed, we didn't want to sit in the stinking room, so ODFOP and I pretty much lived in our bedroom for all those years.

Eating dinner, watching telly, arguing, sleeping and dressing, all in one room.

I understand that lots of people do that when they start out in independent life, house sharing etc. But we had a *four*-bedroomed house, **and** we were in our *forties* **and** I was paying the *mortgage* for a four bedroomed house.

Every room was packed to the rafters with my parents and the family's accumulated "stuff" over thirty plus years, plus the stuff from my/our house.

Every inch of the house needed clearing out, stripping back and starting again. It needed re-wiring, a new boiler, new heating, new kitchen and bathroom, re-plastering, new flooring, and redecorating.

At varying times during those long and at times torturous years, I had begged both ODFOP and my father to agree to selling it, so I could just get out.

Both said "No". Both were actively *hating* each other, but neither of them would "*give in*".

To be fair, it was only my father that could stop us legally selling the house, but ODFOP would not consider us just renting somewhere else to try and save my sanity...

There were times that I *hated* both of them.

A few years ago, my father was diagnosed with Alzheimer's, and his mobility and agility were getting progressively worse. With Alzheimer's, comes the need to be gracious and accommodating of someone who doesn't always think to clean up after themselves.

ODFOP was convinced that my father was doing everything *on purpose*, using his "Alzheimer's" as an excuse to be even more lazy than he already was (which was pretty lazy to be honest).

ODFOP's anger and intolerance ramped up from level 10, to level 90.

My level of covering up for my father's transgressions ramped up from level 20 to level 100.

I was constantly on high alert, looking out for something that was out of place, not cleaned properly, or obvious to ODFOP that my father hadn't done something.

ODFOP would **look** for things to complain about.

- The pantry door wasn't shut, letting the cold in. Lazy fucker.
- Crumbs from a scone or a sandwich on the countertop in the kitchen. Obstinate wanker.
- The toilet has poo stains in the pan. Disgusting c***.
- The Lounge door left often and cigar smoke all over the house. Selfish fucking twat.

My anxiety on the way home from work increased with each train station. What did I need to look out for? What mood would ODFOP be in? Would dad want to talk to me when I had so much to run around and cover up?

I was living in a bedroom with a man who had no hesitation in sharing his bad mood or criticising my father to me - constantly. I learned to live with adrenalin, taking the blame for a million things that ODFOP would find unacceptable and try to blame my father for.

He would let me take the blame, and I would think I was covering it all ok, and then every six months or so he would lose his temper with me and scream that he knew I was covering for "my fucking wanker of a father" - who was inevitably just across the hall in bed (and not deaf).

The house, and my sanity were both barely-holding-it-together hideous dumps. For me, the answer to pretty much any question was "Yes, I will have another glass of wine, thank you". I would have a bottle of wine a night, sometimes more. Very occasionally, less.

Eventually, my father needed his own bathroom, and I couldn't stand the house as it was anymore. ODFOP and I had talked before about whether we would just sell the house to someone who wanted to do it up or do it ourselves and reap some of the financial and comfort, rewards. Neither of us had ever done anything like that before, we were both absolutely and completely shit at anything DIY. The prospect was huge and very daunting.

Luckily, we both have good credit ratings and the bank happily threw money at us. We planned to build a huge bedroom suite in the loft space, an en-suite for my father, an office, and a big glass extension out the back.

We were going to make this house frigging *spectacular*.

Oh, my fucking Christ. There was **so much** STUFF to sort out. Since 1979 when we first walked into this house, **nothing** had ever left, only come in.

Broken beds and chairs in the loft, a million old magazines, books, glassware from my grandparents, school and growing up stuff for 2 of us kids. My mum's art stuff, several dinner services, half empty pots of paints. Suitcase after suitcase of old clothes and shoes.

The garage was piled to the ceiling.

ODFOP would have just thrown it **ALL** out. In fact, I am pretty sure he chucked a lot of stuff when I wasn't there.

My father had no interest in organising anything, but whenever I cajoled him into sorting through some things, he would want to keep **everything**.

It was painful. ODFOP would chuck it in the skip. I would pull it out. Dad would want to keep it exactly where it was.

There were some lovely times as well. When there was no ODFOP telling me to "get on with it" and no dad to persuade, I could go through some old photos of us all growing up, holidays, my lovely mum, or read my school reports and just quietly reminisce.

But mostly it was just painful.

We found a wonderful company called Moduloft to design our gorgeous new second floor bedroom suite. They'd build it all off-site and bring it to the house on the back of big lorries. They'd simply take the roof of our house and plonk these new modules on instead. Much less mess and disruption.

Fabulous. We'll have it. Now we just need the planning permission. No problem! They've never been turned down before, every council loves what they do. Very green and eco-friendly.

Submission made, eight weeks to wait. Very excited.

Application refused.

NoOOooOoooOOOoOOoo! Roof height was too high. Out of character with the road. fuckermutterbollockmutterwank.

Redrawn, a metre taken off the height, a smaller but still fabulous bedroom suite. Submitted. Eight weeks to wait. Very excited, tiny bit apprehensive.

Application refused. Roof *still* too high.

Still out of character with the rest of the road

WTF??? we took a metre off the height!! We'll appeal. Fuckers.

Take photos of 30 other styles of house in the road, no two the same, lots of loft extensions, huge pleading letter accompanying. Examples of precedents set within the council. Sure-fire winner here.

Much confidence and patting on backs.

Submitted. Three months wait.

Appeal not upheld. Out of keeping with the sodding as-eclectic-as-you-can-get character of the tossing road.

All this had taken nearly a year.

We gave up. Gutted.

By this time, we had started the back extension. We basically had the bottom back of the house removed and pushed out by four metres and walled in Georgian windows and French doors topped off with a glass ceiling.

The dust and the dirt and the setbacks and the extra money to fix stuff was just *mind blowing*. Practically every stage had a set-back and an additional £1 - 2,000 to fix it.

I wanted a glass ceiling because I wanted to see and hear the rain. That's *all* I was thinking of.

Not one person - not the architect, the conservatory sales people, the builders **or** ODFOP said before everything was ready to go - "do you think it might be a *bit hot* in the summer?"

No-one. All I was ever thinking about was the rain.

The bamboo flooring was laid by complete cowboys and within weeks it was buckling badly. The plastering cracked. The kitchen company closed for a month for their holidays.

Finally, it was done.

And we had a mini heatwave.

Sweet baby cheeses. It was **roasting**. It was like *nothing* I have ever experienced before, not even Luxor in July. It was so bad that ODFOP bought a huge mobile air conditioning unit. It was the size of an industrial washing machine and just as noisy. But we *loved* it. We would both be sat there like dogs with their head of the car window, just facing the cool wind, for hours.

Then it was time for the garage to be knocked down and the side extension to start.

Luckily, we had brilliant builders who did an amazing job. Knocking through was hideously dusty, and then everything needed to be decorated, but we managed to squeeze in two en-suites and get it all done relatively set-back free.

While we were knocking through and decorating, my father moved into a rest bite care home for 6 weeks. It was a horrible place we found out. He had things stolen, they shaved his beard and moustache off without asking him, he didn't get any exercise at all, he was wheeled everywhere in a wheelchair, so his legs pretty much gave up. He had no bedroom to come home to yet and so it was awful just leaving him there. My sister, in the end found a lovely place near her in Essex. His dementia was dramatically worse, and he still wasn't exercising so his legs were very weak.

We made the decision that he couldn't come back to this house. He couldn't have got up and down the stairs anymore and living in his bedroom wasn't a good option. He had already been living in his bedroom while all the work on the back extension was going on and it just wasn't safe for him to be stuck up there if anything happened to him.

It was a massive relief to be honest. I know it sounds awful and uncaring, but the thought of him being here with the house just done and ODFOP being even more precious than he was when it was a dump, had been giving me nightmares.

We decided *we* would have the lovely bedroom that had been dad's as it had a beautiful en-suite, something that neither of us had had before. We made it a proper tranquil haven, and I loved it.

The house done, we threw a big Sunday party on the bank holiday weekend in the summer. We had an ice cream machine, a barbecue chef, a candyfloss machine and a photo-booth.

It was a gorgeous hot day and we put bunting out along the front of the house and all our neighbours and lots of friends and family came. Family that I hadn't seen since mum's funeral. It was soo good to see everyone. It was a wonderful day. Everyone went around the house and oohed and aared, lots of people had their photos taken in wigs and moustaches. Everyone had lots of food and lots to drink. There was loads of laughter and lots of happy kids running around, high on too much ice cream and candyfloss. It was a great way to mark the end of the year and a half of building work.

Now finally, it was going to be just me and ODFOP alone in a house that I *finally* loved.

About time.

That's when the photo of me and ODFOP was taken. The one where he cut me out and put it as his profile picture on *that* website.

I had **loved** that photo.

But now, when I think about it *without* the rose-tinted glasses, it took me 20 minutes to cajole him into coming to the photo booth with me, 5 minutes to persuade him to wear the pink heart shaped sunglasses and more than one attempt to get him to smile. It wasn't one of us smiling that I loved though, it was the one where we were both in pink heart shaped sunglasses and pulling tongues out at the camera.

It was a fraction of a second in a photo booth.

We looked like a fun couple. A couple that laughed a lot, and *really* got on well. I looked at that photo and thought, "it looks like we're great together" ergo we *are* great together.

I now that have that beautiful tranquil bedroom to **myself**.

Well, me and five cats.

XXII. ODFOP HAS A GIRLFRIEND

It appears that this whole experience, the experience of having the opportunity to reinvent myself as a competent, capable, confident and most importantly, much *smaller* new woman, is also about me discovering there is in fact a trap door at the bottom of this pit of despair that I am currently inhabiting.

I *knew* he was going out on dates. That heartbreak was even healing a little. I was coming to terms with the fact that he said "there's something missing from my life" to me, and that was his way of telling me that he wanted to go out on dates.

You may recall I rather lost my nut at him in a terribly awful drunken way when I first found out.

The new sober me is more magnanimous and doesn't want him to feel he has put his future on hold because I got myself fat and feeling very unattractive.

So, he could date.

It's not about being jealous. It really isn't. I don't want him back now and I don't think even I love him anymore.

Writing this blog has reminded me and crystallised for me what a complete and utter selfish wanker he has been, and I have let him, because I thought I was lucky to have him.

I really honest-to-God thought that I was the lucky one. At his very best ODFOP is romantic, charming, generous, funny and kind. He *always* held my hand in public (except maybe for the last 9 months or so), he'd goose me in Tesco's, and would try and snog me at the checkout - very public displays of affection - I thought I was the luckiest woman to have that.

But, without the rose-tinted glasses of Lalala, the very best of him was about 5% of the time. I just made it feel like it was 95% of the time. Enlarge the good, minimise the bad.

I **am** sad about the end of us, because it feels like a failure. My insecure me is screaming that I failed to keep him interested, and he is a man that would rather wait until the bitter end before making any life changing decisions. He was **at** the bitter end with me.

However, writing this blog and all the fabulous support I have received since I have bared my soul to the internet, friends and family has given me strength. Strength to look at the truth. Strength to stare at my gut wrenching pain and actually *examine* it.

Lalala has been banned from the Craft Room. She still has a big part to play in my life, but the girl needs *boundaries*. No more ignoring pain, no more ignoring Hoam. Equals, with joint decision-making rights.

So, my pain. What does it really consist of? Is there jealousy there? There is some. But it's not jealousy of his new girlfriend. I know she is getting the charming, generous, romantic, witty ODFOP right now, and that's lovely. She's over 50 as well, and so has probably been through her own shit too. I hope she enjoys this time with him, but has the maturity that I didn't, to not put up with his controlling shit. I think my jealousy is that he is in a position to go "out there" and he has already found someone of particular interest, that he likes and wants to spend all his spare time with.

Today was the day someone came to view the house. We had planned to go to the storage unit when the viewing was happening, to sort out stuff that is still in there. He wasn't going out today.

I had been to the farm shop earlier and bought loads of vegetables. I met him at the storage place, and we brought 5 crates of stuff home to go through.

Except he didn't want to go through them today. He went straight upstairs. He came down 20 minutes later and asked me "so, what are your plans for the rest of the afternoon?".

Normally I just answer questions, but I decided to do an ODFOP. "why are you asking?" I said.

"just want to know, that's all"

"why? what are your plans?"

"well, you look like you've bought stuff for a roast dinner. Are you planning on making a roast dinner?"

"no - so what are your plans?"

"well, if you're not planning on making a roast dinner, I might go out then"

"you'd better go out then".

Within 2 minutes he was out the door

"see you a bit later then" he said.

"try not to crash your car and die" I said after the front door was shut.

I know. Really crap thing to say, especially if he does crash his car and die.

He'd been out on a 12-hour date with this woman yesterday and told me he was seeing her again on Tuesday this week.

She lives in Bromley apparently and works in an office. I did ask. I wanted to know. I wanted to get as hurt as I could - get it over and done with, rather than death by a thousand tiny heartbreaks. He was smiling when he was talking about her, but maybe it was because he felt awkward.

So, he has gone out to visit his new girlfriend, and I am at home by myself, again, crying onto my laptop.

So, there is a little bit of jealousy there. I admit to that, but not the kind of jealousy I thought it would be. He is no longer a prize catch as far as I am concerned. He has done too much that hurt me, and he didn't care enough about me to stop doing it.

There is lots of self-pity. I feel *thrown away*. Discarded and unwanted, by someone who isn't even a prize catch anymore.

Super ouch. To be thrown away by someone who is out of my league, that's kind of understandable and self-pity is expected. Thrown away by a selfish wanker, damn it, that *hurts*.

My lovely first husband said there was a saying in Egypt which encapsulated the feeling of not being wanted by someone you don't think even deserves you. I must ask him what that saying is.

My very low self-esteem has been fed by ODFOP getting a girlfriend so soon after our split. I am shouting at my low self-esteem

"NO! His actions do NOT mean I am worthless - his actions do not affect me at all".

But the tears and the snotty nose still come. The swirling hot ache in my ribs is still here, even though I am telling myself **I am worth more**.

I was sobbing to my sister on the phone in my car today as I drove to the farm shop. Feeling very hard done by and undeserving of such pain and torment. *I knew* it wasn't jealousy I was feeling, I had no ill will toward this woman at all.

My angry hurt tears were there because - **well, Karma - where the fuck are you??** He has been nothing short of a selfish c word for most of our relationship. We split up, and he has not cried one tear (I don't cry really, he said - oh yes, he does though, I have seen him cry a hundred times before).

He joined a scamming sex website and I told him, saving him hundreds of pounds and possibly a bit of pride, and I get no thanks for that, I get told he meant what he said. I forgive him, and the following week ask him to consider us getting back together. He tells me he doesn't love me. I go away and cry out of sight. I am friendly with him because I hate a horrible atmosphere. I cook and chat. He goes and sits in his own lounge and shuts the door, even though we are often watching the same thing on the television. I lose my shit and frighten him when he has his first date - he continues to date anyway. I decide I can't stop him going after his future and if he moves out it will cost us both more money and I am frankly completely skint paying the loans and the mortgage on this house.

Two weeks later he has a girlfriend and he can't wait to see her, so after less than 18 hours apart, he drives off to see her again. I am sitting here with tears and snot streaming down my face, every muscle aching from going to the gym yesterday, and I'm **still fat**.

Why is he having such an easy time of this? He hasn't suffered *at all* - yet **he** is the selfish bastard.

I *want him to be suffering*, to feel emotional pain, or indeed **any** pain would do. Just something that marks the end of a long relationship with me - anything.

But of course, it can't come from me. That makes me the bad one.

I just want the Universe to put the boot in. Is that so much to ask??

I *did* do something awful when I knew he was out on that first date. He had a full bottle of expensive red wine open on the side. He'd just spent £500 on a new rug for himself....

oh yes, I did.

I just tipped it over and walked away. It felt **good**. I told him one of the cats was in his room.

I want to tell him that I lied about our sex life for the whole of our 17-year relationship.

I want to be like Rachel in Friends when she shouts after Ross "It's **not** that common, it **doesn't** happen to every guy, and it **IS** a big deal!".

ODFOP's ex-wife quite bluntly told him that he wasn't well endowed and that he wasn't that skilled - she was out to hurt him of course. But, me being me, made a **huge** thing of how *amazing* he was in every possible area of intimacy.

He just had to touch a boob and I would quiver and melt all over the place. Never had the world seen such a match made in heaven. We fitted together so perfectly. I faked **so** much. Who is the mug here? I sabotaged my own sexual gratification to boost his ego. What an idiot.

So, I won't tell him I lied to him, because I think that says more about me than it does about him, and also, I really don't want to hurt him. I want something *else* to hurt him.... Not physically, really. Physical pain heals too quickly. I really want him to suffer for something emotionally, and for me to **not** be there to make it better for him.

Universe, are you frigging listening?

If I get hit by a bus tomorrow, you'll know why.

XXIII. ODFOP – Gaslighter Extraordinaire

I have today been introduced to a new word by a fabulous friend.

It is a revelation to me and so I have to tell you about it immediately.

The mind games that ODFOP played with/on me, *has a name all of its own.* **It even has its own wiki page!**

I feel like I have had a mystery ailment for years and no one could tell me what was wrong with me and suddenly *I am diagnosed.*

It means I am not the only one in the world. I am not alone. This is a *known* thing. Oh, the relief.

Oh, what a complete fucker ODFOP is.

ODFOP is a skilled **Gaslighter**.

It took me *years* to even recognise that he didn't argue fairly. I just assumed I must be in the wrong - because he was *so sure* of himself and what he was saying. I was an idiot who couldn't keep up with him.

I remember the day that I noticed for the first time that he was changing and twisting the argument, so I was 100% wrong and he was the innocent victim of my venomous accusatory blame casting.

I apologise for the mind-numbing banality of this little vignette, it's dull and insignificant, but you my lovely one reader may come across a Gaslighter in your future, and I want you to be on the lookout, because they are stealers of confidence and conviction, and **must never be allowed to do this to you**. It is a hideous horrible skill.

We were going to the cinema and to have something to eat afterwards in Greenwich. I said to ODFOP "three and a half hours should be enough shouldn't it?" he looked at his watch and said "Yes, the film is two hours, plus all the trailers and then something to eat, that should be fine" so off I went to the parking metre to get a ticket.

The parking fees in Greenwich are set so that you must put the money in for the whole hour or it won't register for any part of that hour at all. I didn't know that as ODFOP **always** got the parking ticket from the machine. The parking metres that I had previously used would give you part of an hour for part of the cost e.g. £1 got you 15 minutes or whatever.

So, I put in enough for three and a half hours. I didn't look at the time on the ticket, I just put it in the car on the dashboard. I should've checked, but I didn't. Off we went to the cinema and then to get something to eat.

We come back to a parking ticket. We had been about three hours and 15 minutes.

"You only got three hours"

"I didn't, I had got three and a half".

I'll spare you the tooing and froing for five minutes of No you didn't, yes, I did.

I picked the ticket up off the dashboard and it **did** only say on time that it was valid for three hours.

Oh shit. One of the *very few* times I was absolutely 100% sure of myself, and therefore argued back, and I was wrong.

Bollocks.

ODFOP was right and I was losing my mind. Except I *knew* I had put in enough money for three and a half hours.

ODFOP was absolutely going off on one telling me I was saying black was white and I was WRONG and because I didn't pay attention, we had got a parking ticket (which I think was about £80 - Greenwich is a bastard for parking ticket fees).

I went and looked at the machine notice board. I saw how much it was for three hours and how much it was for four hours. I looked on the ticket which showed that I **had** put in enough for three and a half hours.

I self-righteously stomped back to him and said "the ticket shows how much I put in the machine - I put in enough for three and a half hours - DON'T tell me I don't know what I am talking about because it's here on the fucking ticket."

He grabbed the ticket off me and looked at it. We then both stomped back to the machine.

By the way, the car park was busy and there was a car waiting to get into our parking spot and they were stopped in such a way that no other car could get past it. We were holding up the car park traffic...

Looking at the noticeboard by the ticket machine, I then read that it only calculates on full hours.

"It says it only calculates in full hours here" I said "I didn't know that" I was calming down and being contrite about the fact I had made a mistake.

"I told you that" he said.

From contrite back to raging. "Oh no you fucking didn't".

"I told you when you took the money from the console that it had to be in full hours"

256

"I asked you if three and a half hours was enough, and you said yes it was - if you knew, why didn't you tell me you can only pay for full hours?"

"Why I am responsible for you not reading the fucking machine details?"

"You are not. I am saying that I told you I was getting three and a half hours and you said that was fine. If you knew that I couldn't do that, why didn't you tell me?"

"so, you're saying I need to check you're absolutely clear on everything you have to do, even tell you how to get a parking ticket from the machine, because if I don't then it's my fault?"

"No, that's not what I am saying. I'm asking why you didn't tell me if you knew - you're saying I am stupid or lazy for not reading the rules of the car park tickets, when you get tickets here every weekend, and this is my first time. If you knew, why didn't you tell me?"

"I've never said you were stupid, or lazy. When did I call you stupid?"

"you didn't, I'm saying that's what it feels like"

"You just said I said you were stupid and lazy - I've never used those words"

"Oh, for fucks sake! This is a fucking parking ticket! We are having a full argument about a fucking parking ticket in the middle of Greenwich car park and we're holding up traffic. I will pay for the fucking fine. Up until this point in time I'd had a lovely day with you, now you're acting like a wanker and I'm miserable - let's just get in the fucking car and go home"

"you said I called you stupid and lazy, and now you're calling me a wanker because you got the wrong parking ticket and you're acting as though this is my fault"

Oh, My Good God. As I was typing that I was reliving it, and 10,000 other occasions where he would twist and turn in an argument and I would end up feeling like I was an unreasonable, unfair, unjust bitch.

I can hand on heart, scouts honour say, in the 17 years we were together, in the heat of an argument, or even after an argument, he **never once** took *any* responsibility for doing *anything* wrong at all. **Not once.**

If he was in the wrong, he would ALWAYS latch on to some insignificant word or phrase and suddenly the whole argument was about that. He would talk over me and reiterate that part about that one word and would never let me get back to the original point. He would then walk off and stop talking to me.

As you know, and as *he* knew very well, I couldn't stand a tense atmosphere. I hated arguing. I desperately wanted my life to be all cuddling up on the sofa and being each other's ally and cheerleader. But, whenever some situation looked like he had done something wrong, and I knew it, it would turn into an argument. I didn't want a row, I just wanted to know that **I** wasn't wrong. I didn't want to *blame* him, God knows we all make mistakes.

One thing I **never** want to change about myself is that I will admit when I am wrong. I will apologise without reservation. I just can't see that there is ever any benefit to *anyone* in trying to blame someone else if I know I've cocked up. Apologising is just the best thing for everyone - how can someone trust me if I don't accept responsibility for my own mistakes?

Why can't ODFOP do that? It doesn't mean *blame*. It means accountability.

He would say to me "you're always looking to blame me, you're always trying to make me apologise, sometimes **no one** is to blame, stuff just happens"

I agree 100% that sometimes stuff just happens. It was his determination to not be accountable for *anything* that made me push for an apology from him. Like the row above, which I have just bashed out on this poor innocent keyboard. I apologise keyboard.

I cried all the way home and he just stayed silent in the car.

"why aren't you even sorry that I am upset?"

"You're the one that gets upset, it's not *my* fault you get upset"

"but we've just had a great afternoon and then we've ended up having a massive argument over something that wasn't anyone's *fault,* but you are so keen to blame me, when you could've prevented me making that error by telling me when I said about the half hour, or if you'd forgotten about it, then it's just one of those stupid things that happens, and we could've just shrugged it off as a bit of a shit thing to happen. But you work so hard to make sure you have no responsibility whatsoever, and you change the focus of the argument that I feel I need to defend myself"

"You're the one that got the ticket, you're the one who said I called you stupid and lazy when I didn't, and now you're telling me I should apologise that you're upset - you're always looking to get me to apologise for everything".

Aaaargh. That little incident was about 10 years ago. It was a mini lightbulb moment for me, and over the years I began to be a little more prepared and call him out on his twisting the truth.

Looking back, I think that made our arguments shorter (as he would storm off) but the silences longer. I wasn't smart or brave enough to be able to deal with the silences.

Either way, he got away with it. Every time.

I am starting to see now, that that's when he would punish me - with the withdrawal of affection, and I would practically beg to get it back. I treated his affection as my self-worth.

Over the years he has created an argument out of nothing at least 1,000 times. I was always left wondering "what just happened? we were fine 10 minutes ago?" He would never want to talk about it so (I thought) we could learn to communicate better.

ODFOP is a very skilled manipulator.

A wonderful friend of mine said because ODFOP dislikes himself so much, he hides it by pointing out flaws in me. Flaws that aren't even flaws. But I took them all as flaws, because he said they were.

Well, of course right about now he would be pointing out that he never used the **word** *flaws*...

Gaslighting. It's got its own bloody Wiki page. It's a known thing. The Wiki page should just say **Gaslighting a.k.a. ODFOPPING.**

Its formal description is - Sociopaths and narcissists frequently use gaslighting tactics. Sociopaths consistently.... exploit others, but typically also are convincing liars, sometimes charming ones, who consistently deny wrongdoing. Thus, some who have been victimized by sociopaths may doubt their own perceptions.

An abuser's ultimate goal is to make their victim second guess their every choice and question their sanity, making them more dependent on the abuser. A tactic which further degrades a target's self-esteem is for the abuser to ignore, then attend to, then ignore the victim again, so the victim lowers their personal bar for what constitutes affection and perceives themselves as less worthy of affection.

What kind of absolute wanker does that to someone they say they love?

And Yes ODFOP, this time I **did** call you a wanker.

XXIV. ODFOP THE CULT LEADER

I said some pretty bad things in my post about wishing karma would kick ODFOP's butt. I think my green-eyed monster prevailed with him pursuing and wooing this new girlfriend. I know at the time, I did desperately want ODFOP to get some negative karma, so I could sit back and gloat.

That's not me. If he fell over onto a custard pie, of course I would laugh until my sides split before trying to pick him up, I'm human after all. But I'm not a gloater.

My wish for his public undoing didn't last long anyway. I have mentioned before my amazing Roar of Unicorns. A fabulous collection of rare women, along with you, who are helping me traverse this previously untrodden path, from bombsite to bombshell.

Gedgster, who is one of these amazing women, pointed out what I just could not see.

ODFOP can't stand being by himself. The man has not been single for more than a week since he was 18. And before that he lived with his parents.

Now, if you've been *really* paying attention, you will know that I would've crawled naked over hot coals to have *not* been single for most of my fertile and attractive years. But, I am still able to understand that if you have effectively *never* been alone for your whole adult life, the prospect of becoming so at 50+, is poo-in-your-pants scary.

It is for me, and I am an old hand at being alone.

I understand, and I sympathise with ODFOP....to an extent.

Since I have had the luxury of reflecting over my 17-year relationship with ODFOP - *sans* rose tinted glasses, to put it bluntly, I am starting to feel a trifle *irked* at him.

I no longer believe that I am heartbroken, but I am in fact, experiencing **withdrawal symptoms.** Similar to those people who manage to escape a cult, like the Moonies, Scientology, or the Cliff Richard Fan Club.

There is pain, jealousy, **so** much self-doubt and wretchedness, and a tiny bit of me **desperate** to get back into his arms and for him to *forgive* me.

Except I know now I was *never* safe with him. He absolutely is someone I should run, screaming with my hands in the air, from. In fact, I came across this amazing song recently, called **Run, by Nicole Sherzinger.** It's about giving advice to next the girlfriend – it's AMAZING. I have learned it word for word – if not note for note... You Tube it. Proper belter of a song.

Over the last 24 hours I have read much *much* more on the this Gaslighting business. I have read some absolute horror stories that make my relationship with ODFOP look like a teenage girls' daydream. But still, in **all** of it, every article, every life story, and every internet page, I see ODFOP's behaviour.

There are three stages to gaslighting in a relationship: idealisation, devaluation and discard.

I was swept off my feet and made to feel like the most precious princess that ever did live.

He *worshipped* me. He *spoiled* me. He repeatedly told me he realised he had *never* been in love before me, and now he knew what **real** love was. He only had eyes for me, even when we were around gorgeous women - I *never* saw him even *glance* at them appreciatively. He was romantic, and so very attentive to my every whim - even when I didn't know my whims were showing.

For a year. Maybe a touch less.

Then the *tiny* criticisms crept in.

I'd hurt his feelings by not saying something, or by talking to someone else too much when we were out.

I'd not asked his opinion on an outfit before I bought it or worn it, or he didn't like the shoes I had bought. The point was, I had hurt him. Just a bit. Nothing to really worry about. He just thought I should know.

Of course, for **me**, that was a red flashing light and a siren going off. To his tiny "hardly worth mentioning" comments, I rallied 110,000,000% to overcompensate for *ever* hurting him. That was the *last* thing I would **ever** want to do.

Oh, frigging bollocks, I was **perfect** for this.

My eagerness to please him meant he hardly had to do *anything* to control me. I got to know "The Look". I learned to pre-empt **The Look** and ensure that I did everything right in order to make him happy. If I missed a cue, or it was something new, I got *The Look* **and** the silent treatment. He wasn't *angry* with me. He was *disappointed* that I didn't care enough. That was a *million times worse* than anger.

I was so lucky to have him, because he *cherished* me. I would have done **anything**. I would have butterflies a lot of the time, *desperate* to make him as happy as he had made me. As time went on, getting to the Nirvana that was his happiness and approval, got increasingly but imperceptibly, harder and more complex.

He didn't even have to *mention* being hurt or disappointed. I *knew*. And I played along. This was a game of Twister that started out being fun and ended up being physically and mentally like trying to put one

266

finger, one toe and a nipple on each of the coloured circles *all at the same time.* There are 24 circles on a Twister mat.

Sometimes I would ask him what I'd done wrong, and he would say "nothing, it's fine" and that would make it 100 times worse for me.

Occasionally he would say "I shouldn't have to tell you - if you don't know yourself..." and the rest of the unsaid sentence would hang in the air, like a bullet coming at Neo in Matrix.

Until I learned not to, I would push it and beg him to let me know, so I could learn and *not do it again*. He would get annoyed and tell me to "stop going on about it", and then **I** had made it **worse for him**.

Early in our relationship, we would go out meeting my friends on a regular basis and I loved it. Finally, I wasn't the Bridget Jones at the dinner party.

In later years, whenever we went out with people I cared about, I was on edge all the time, I would be *willing* them to phrase their sentences in a certain way, or not challenge anything ODFOP said.

We would laugh and hold hands and kiss in front of them but, 90% of the time I would've seen in his face that I had done *something* wrong, and inside I wanted to cry. I had let him down, and I didn't know what I had missed.

It was even worse when it wasn't me that had upset him, if it was a friend that said or did something. I would desperately try and make it ok for him by light heartedly saying they meant it as a joke, or taking the blame myself, as I didn't want to lose that friend.

If ODFOP made a judgement on them, then that was it. I knew they were lost to me, eventually.

Over maybe 5 or 6 years, most of my friends (or their partner), made some impossible-to-know mistake as far as he was concerned, and that was that. He couldn't forgive them, and it was "up to me" if I wanted to carry on seeing them...

Sometimes I would for a while, and he would drop in a comment about me being "weak" or a "walk-over" as I hadn't seen what he saw.

And so, I stopped seeing them.

That included my sister, who I was closer to than anyone in the world. We didn't talk for nearly **10 years**. ODFOP had me believing that she was manipulative, scheming, selfish and I was better off without her. He was good, because I really *really* did believe it.

I lost touch with all my family except my brother. I was allowed to keep him because he was *useful*. He could mend things and he was inexpensive. But I had to dance around ODFOP and cover up for my brother doing (perfectly normal) things that would upset him. I couldn't risk losing my brother as well. He had turned me against my father who was living with us, and both my sisters. I **needed** my brother.

He didn't like his own sister or his mum either. I even fell out with his sister defending him. How dare she verbally attack my man?

Just to interject here, it is hard to type when you are constantly face-palming yourself....

My forever was with ODFOP. We didn't need family, and we would make new friends, together.

Except we very rarely did. ODFOP came to our relationship with one friend, Keith, who we saw twice.

One or two couples prevailed, thank God. One couple was my BM and her husband. You may recall the husband is also a constant absorber and seeker of knowledge, so there was someone who was actually a challenge for ODFOP. ODFOP respected him and wanted to please and impress him.

ODFOP would choose him over me every day of the week.

I recall a time when the four of us went to Galway Bay Oyster Festival together. It was our first trip away with another couple. Possibly about 15 years ago. Something I don't think any of us knew at the time, was that BM's husband could be a little blunt and cross if he is was drinking and something pissed him off.

We were in a busy bustling restaurant, all drinking quite a lot of wine and having a fabulous time. ODFOP went to the loo and I said something that was taken as negative about ODFOP. We were all quite drunk and I don't remember. I loved him and was delighted with him, but it was entirely possible that I did. BM's husband rounded on me and had a go. I was so shocked as we had all been laughing seconds earlier. Anyway, as it is with alcohol, shock turned to tears. ODFOP returned from the toilet and I was drunk and sobbing. I went outside for a cigarette (yes, I know...).

ODFOP didn't come out. My BM did. She was lovely. ODFOP stayed in the restaurant with BM's husband chatting happily. I couldn't go back in to the restaurant and so the bill was paid, and we walked away. ODFOP stayed by the side of BM's husband. He didn't even come to check if I was ok. Seeing him not defend me, or even comfort me, made me cry even more. My poor BM was in the middle, walking with a sobbing drunk mess of a me and her husband and ODFOP walking ahead, chatting and laughing and continuing the lovely evening we had all been having.

That was the first time I discovered he would never defend me, or stand up for me, or even just *be* with me if I was hurt by someone else.

My nephew (going through his angry teenage years) threatened me with a knife once. ODFOP actually left the room. He said it was a "family matter".

On the plus side, ODFOP was a very good gift giver.

Christmas Eve, for many years was spent at my BM's.

ODFOP would be collecting presents for them all year. He would buy special wrapping paper for each individual and wrap everything at work.

He would *never* tell me what he had bought them. The label said from both of us, but these gifts weren't from us, they were from *him*.

His favourite time possibly in his life was sitting back and watching them open their presents, and either them seeing the connection and the thoughtfulness, or him explaining the connection. He was very happy then. These people that he looked up to and possibly saw as slightly out of his league, were emotional and so very touched by his thoughtfulness.

I remember our first Christmas together. I had to stop opening presents because I was too overwhelmed. Everything I had mentioned, from the moment we got together (or even before) had been stored in his mind and converted into a gift.

It felt like I'd won the lottery.

Of course, I had done something similar for him. Or I *thought* I had. Probably £1,000 each year spent on things I thought he would love. He was **never** even half as thrilled as I thought he would be. And then nothing I bought him really got used. Things stayed in the boxes and just got put away, to be given to charity two years later. I was left feeling like it was obvious I didn't care about him enough to get his gifts right.

He wore a Paul Smith scarf I bought him. Every time he wore it I was jumping for joy inside. It was almost as good as one of the half a dozen time he said my name.

I spent so much of my time building up ODFOP's confidence and self-esteem, that I didn't take care of my own, and I let ODFOP trample all over them.

I think his terrible insecurity and lack of confidence is masked by his intellect, and by me believing I was so very lucky to have him.

He absolutely *relished* it when I didn't know the meaning of a word and would ask him, or I used a word incorrectly in a sentence. He would *delight* in correcting and mocking me. I responded to this by trying to think of a word a couple of times a week that I could ask him the meaning of. I saw him transform in front of my eyes. His chest would puff out, he would smile with his mouth and his eyes. I was happy he felt clever, it didn't matter that it was at my expense.

In the end I really felt that his, some spoken, some implied, criticisms of me were realistic or possibly even generous of him. (Jesus, implied or inferred - I write the word and I got a knot in my stomach - that was one of ODFOP's favourite misuses to mock)

I believed he was the only person who knew the real, terribly flawed, me. And he stayed with me *despite* my failings. Whaddaguy! He deserved more than me, so I had better be everything he wants, then he may, if I am **very** lucky, stay around.

Me and my sister making up and getting back together I think was the beginning of the end for me and ODFOP.

I had defied him and **was never letting her go again** and that REALLY disappointed him.

I had broken the seal that bonded just us together and there were parts of my life that he was losing control of.

Boy oh boy, was he going to make me pay.

Printed in Great Britain
by Amazon